Private Recipes from Private Clubs

BEVERLY ANDERSON BARBOUR

Published by
CAHNERS BOOKS INTERNATIONAL, INC.
221 Columbus Ave., Boston, Massachusetts 02116
Publishers of Institutions/VF Magazine

ACKNOWLEDGEMENT

We are indebted to Mr. Johnson Poor, publisher of *Club Management* magazine, for permission to use the recipes that appear in this book. This material has been previously copyrighted by Commerce Publishing Co. and *Club Management.*

ISBN 0-8436-2095-1

Printed in the United States of America

Cover and inside photos by: John Thos. Grubell of the *Culinary Institute of America*

Contents

Introduction

Private clubs differ from most restaurants in that they have a relatively unchanging clientele who own the club and regard it as an extension of their own homes.

With the same people coming back to the club to eat day after day and week after week, clubs must offer good food and service, coupled with variety. Boredom sets in hard and fast—particularly at the table.

The nice consequences of this are high standards and interesting food. Some of the best food in the United States is found in private clubs. We are fortunate that many of the clubs noted for their outstandingly fine cuisine have shared their recipes with us and with you.

Their recipes have been set forth both in small portions which can be prepared for a la carte service or for the family and in larger quantities for professional use or for the use of the home chef who is entertaining a sizable group of people.

In instances in which the recipe calls for a sauce or an ingredient which is really another prepared dish, a recipe for the missing ingredient has been supplied in the chapter entitled "Recipe References."

We are very grateful to the managers and the chefs of the clubs whose recipes are given here. The recipes were gathered, over a period of 8 years of personal visits to clubs, from interviews with the managers and chefs for *Club Management* magazine. It was good of them to share their secrets, and you will enjoy their good dishes as much as the club members and I have.

Private Recipes from Private Clubs

The Army and Navy Club

Washington, D. C.

While serving in Puerto Rico in 1898, old General Wilson, a veteran of the Civil War, thought it would make good sense if the Spanish would surrender and prevent further spillage of Spanish and American blood. An innovative man, he had a sheet tied to a pole and instructed an orderly to carry it ahead of his adjutant, then Captain Tasker H. Bliss. Both the orderly and the captain were probably as white as the sheet, but they marched on carrying a note from General Wilson to the Spanish commander. The Spanish honored the bedsheet but penned a note back that if the American commander wished to prevent further bloodshed he had damned well better stay put!

The pole, the bedsheet, and the handwritten Spanish note are among the historic military mementos that make the Washington, D. C. Army and Navy Club a fascinating place to dine. Membership is limited to officers of any branch of the American military establishment, the Coast Guard, foreign service officers, military attaches of foreign governments with legations in Washington, NATO force officers, and the combined chiefs of staff. Nonmembers of both sexes may come as guests . . . and the food is well worth the effort of riding in on someone else's mettle or medal.

JAVANESE EGGS

(An unusual buffet item—inexpensive and "different")

YIELD:	6 PORTIONS	24 PORTIONS	
INGREDIENTS			**METHOD**
Eggs, hard-cooked	6	24	1. Cut hard-cooked eggs in half and arrange on a platter.
Tomatoes, peeled, chopped	1	4	2. Combine tomatoes, curry powder, and peanut butter to make a sauce.
Curry Powder	1/4 tsp.	1 tsp.	
Peanut Butter	1 tbsp.	1/4 cup	3. Pour the sauce over the eggs and garnish with parsley.
Parsley, chopped	1 tsp.	1/4 cup	

CANAPES PADEN

(These hot, sharply flavored appetizers are quickly made)

YIELD:	1 CUP	1 QUART	
INGREDIENTS			**METHOD**
Blue Cheese	4 oz.	1 lb.	1. Combine cheese, oil, cayenne pepper, and worcestershire in a blender to make a smooth paste.
Salad Oil	1/3 cup	1-1/3 cups	
Cayenne Pepper	to taste	to taste	
Worcestershire Sauce	2/3 tsp.	1 tbsp.	2. Spread on untoasted side of bite-sized bread squares and broil until bubbling. Watch closely as the cheese mixture burns quickly.
White Bread Squares, toasted on 1 side	50	200	
			3. Serve hot.

CUCUMBER STRIPS ★

(A perfect dish for the long, nearly seedless European cucumber)

YIELD:	2 CUPS	10 CUPS	
INGREDIENTS			**METHOD**
Cucumbers			1. Cut cucumbers in finger-length strips.
MARINADE			
Vinegar	1 cup	5 cups	2. Marinate in a solution of half vinegar and and half water with granulated sugar and dried red peppers added. Heat over medium heat for 10 minutes to expand the flavor.
Water	1 cup	5 cups	
Granulated Sugar	1 tbsp.	5 tbsp.	
Red Peppers, Dried	1 tsp.	5 tsp.	

★ See picture, facing page.

CUCUMBER STRIPS

Superior
Farming Co.

FRIED BANANAS ★

(Serve as an accompaniment to curry or cook at tableside and flambe for a dessert)

YIELD: 4 PORTIONS

INGREDIENTS		METHOD
Bananas, slightly green	4	1. Cut bananas in half lengthwise.
Brown Sugar	1/4 cup	2. Sprinkle with brown sugar and confection-
Confectioners' Sugar	1 tbsp.	ers' sugar and pan fry until brown but still
Butter	1/4 cup	firm. Be careful not to break or mash the
		bananas.

NOTE   After cooking, bananas may be flambeed with high-proof rum and/or Grand Marnier.   Serve with vanilla ice cream and whipped cream lightly touched with an orange-flavored liqueur.

FRIED RICE (NASI GORENG)

(An Indonesian favorite combining meat, rice, and shreds of omelet)

YIELD: 6 PORTIONS   24 PORTIONS

INGREDIENTS			METHOD
Green Onions, finely chopped	1/2 cup	2 cups	1. Fry onions, celery, and pimiento in oil; season with Sambal Nasi Goreng.
Celery, finely sliced	1/2 cup	2 cups	2. Add meat or poultry; season lightly with soy sauce. Drain well and mix into rice.
Pimiento, finely chopped	1/4 cup	1 cup	3. Reheat and serve combined with, or on top of, shredded omelet strips.
Salad Oil	2 tbsp.	1/2 cup	
Sambal Nasi Goreng*	to taste	to taste	
Beef, Pork, *or* Chicken, finely diced	1 cup	1 qt.	
Soy Sauce	to taste	to taste	
Rice, cooked, cooled	3 cups	3 qt.	
Omelet, 2 egg (recipe, p. 232)	1	4	

*Sambal Nasi Goreng may be purchased in gourmet shops or specialty food shops.

★ See picture, facing page.

FRIED BANANAS

Castle and
Cooke Foods,
Inc.

SATE

(Pass these at cocktail time—they're a good way to use small amounts of meat)

YIELD:	6 SMALL SKEWERS	24 SMALL SKEWERS

INGREDIENTS			METHOD
Chicken, Turkey,			1. Marinate meat or fowl in combined soy sauce, lime juice, Bumbu Sate, and vegetable oil for several hours or overnight.
or Pork, cut in			
1/4-inch cubes	1 cup	1 qt.	
Soy Sauce	1 tbsp.	1/4 cup	
Fresh Lime Juice	1 tsp	4 tsp.	2. Place 4 or 5 pieces on bamboo skewers; broil.
Bumbu Sate Powder*	1/2 tsp.	2 tsp.	
Vegetable Oil	to cover	to cover	3. Serve with a sauce made from coconut milk and Bumbu Sate to taste.
Coconut Milk**	1 cup	1 qt.	
Bumbu Sate Powder	to taste	to taste	

*Bumbu Sate Powder can be purchased in gourmet shops or specialty food shops.
**Plain milk can be used. Or, coconut milk can be made by steeping shredded coconut in boiling water and simmering for 30 minutes. A canned coconut milk called "CoCo Lopez" is also available.

INDONESIAN SATE ★

(Small cubes of pork or chicken marinated, broiled, and served with an exotic sauce— an unusual appetizer or to serve with rice for lunch)

YIELD	6 PORTIONS	24 PORTIONS

INGREDIENTS			METHOD
Lean Pork *or* Chicken,			1. Marinate pork or chicken in combined soy sauce, lime juice, and green onions for 12 to 24 hours.
cut in bite-sized			
cubes	1-1/2 lb.	6 lb.	
Soy Sauce	1 cup	1 qt.	2. Thread onto skewers and broil slowly, turning once or twice.
Lime Juice	1/4 cup	1 cup	
Green Onions, chopped	1/4 cup	1 cup	3. Serve dipped into Peanut Butter Sauce, made by combining the peanut butter, condensed milk, and Sambal Nasi Goreng until smooth.
PEANUT BUTTER SAUCE			
Peanut Butter	1/2 cup	2 cups	
Condensed Milk	1/4 cup	1 cup	
Sambal Nasi Goreng			
or			
Sambal Oelik*	to taste	to taste	

*Sambal Nasi Goreng or Sambal Oelik can be purchased in gourmet shops or specialty food shops.
★ See picture, facing page.

INDONESIAN SATE

Peanut
Associates, Inc.

CREPES SUZETTE

(Tender crepes filled with Orange Butter and flambeed with an orange-flavored liqueur; the crepes can be made well ahead and stored or frozen)

YIELD:	6 PORTIONS	24 PORTIONS
INGREDIENTS		
BATTER		
Flour	1/3 cup	1-1/3 cups
Egg	1	4
Egg Yolk	1	4
Salt	1/8 tsp.	1/2 tsp.
Butter, melted	2 tbsp.	1/2 cup (1/4 lb.)
Whole Milk	1/4 cup	1 cup
ORANGE BUTTER		
Butter	6 tbsp.	3/4 lb.
Granulated Sugar	3/4 cup	3 cups
Orange, grated rind of	1	4
Curacao	1 tbsp.	2 oz. (1/4 cup)
TO FLAMBE CREPES		
Butter	6 tbsp.	
Granulated Sugar	3/4 cup	
Orange, grated rind of	1	
Orange Juice	1/2 cup	
Brandy	1/2 cup	
Grand Marnier *or*		
Curacao	2 oz.	

METHOD

1. Combine ingredients and beat until smooth; add additional milk to make batter the consistency of light cream. Cover the bowl and refrigerate for at least 1 hour to thicken the batter.
2. Cook crepes on both sides in a clean buttered pan, making as thin as possible by tilting pan so that batter rolls evenly to barely coat bottom.
3. Fill finished crepes with Orange Butter.
4. Combine Orange Butter Ingredients and spread crepes with the mixture.
5. Fold crepes in half, then in half again, to obtain triangles. Flambe crepes at tableside.
6. In crepe pan, melt butter and stir in sugar, orange rind and juice, and brandy. Cook until syrupy. Place folded crepes in sauce and ladle the sauce over the crepes to heat them well.
7. Pour warmed orange-flavored liqueur over the crepes and ignite. Shake the pan so that the flame spreads over the entire surface. Serve hot.

Atlanta Athletic Club

Atlanta, Georgia

The Atlanta Athletic Club has three clubhouses and is, in effect, three clubs—a city club with a downtown Atlanta address, a country club located in the suburbs, and a yacht club. The one thing that all three have in common is good food with a touch of the South in its flavor.

One of the most successful of the club's parties was billed as a "Night in Georgia" and featured a true down-South, mouth-watering menu served in the downtown club, which had gone rustic for the evening. Kerosene lanterns on red-checked tablecloths illuminated tables set "family-style" for 10 each. No seating choice was allowed; tables were filled as the bodies appeared, and as soon as a table was completely occupied, a waiter wheeled out a large crock of vegetable soup, which he proceeded to ladle into old crockery bowls.

The soup was followed by fried chicken, country ham, sliced beef, dumplings, fresh cream-style corn, pole beans, potatoes, candied yams, black-eyed peas, and pinto beans. Loaves of freshly baked bread were on each table, as were corn pone, hot biscuits, and pitchers of fresh buttermilk. There were also platters of sliced tomatoes, raw onion rings, and pickles. Peach and blackberry cobblers were served for dessert.

Old-fashioned food is fun, and the club is modern enough to include it on its daily menu as well as at party time.

FROZEN LAYER CAKE WITH EGGNOG SAUCE

(Cinnamon-Sugar Icing with macaroon crunch and pecans frosts a cake layered with whipped ice cream. The frozen cake goes to the table with Eggnog Sauce)

YIELD:	1 CAKE	6 CAKES
INGREDIENTS		
Cake Flour, sifted	4 cups	5 lb.
Granulated Sugar	2 cups	6 lb.
Milk Powder	4-1/2 tbsp.	8 oz. (1-3/4 cup)
Salt	1 tsp.	2 oz.
Baking Powder	1/2 tsp.	3/4 oz.
Shortening	1 cup plus 1-1/2 tbsp.	3-1/4 lb.
Water	3/4 cup	4-1/2 cups
Eggs	2/3 cup	3 lb., 8 oz.
Vanilla	1 tsp.	2 tbsp.
Egg Shade *or* Yellow Food Coloring	as needed	as needed
CINNAMON SUGAR ICING		
Confectioners' Sugar	3 cups	5 lb.
Shortening	1/3 cup	1 lb.
Water	1/4 cup	12 oz. (1-1/2 cups)
Vanilla	1 tsp.	2 tbsp.
Cinnamon	2 tsp.	2 tbsp.
Nutmeg	1/8 tsp.	1/2 tsp.
DECORATION		
Macaroons, crushed	1/3 cup	2 cups
Pecans, chopped	2 tbsp.	3/4 cup
WHIPPED ICE CREAM		
Ice Cream	1 qt.	6 qt.
EGGNOG SAUCE		
Vanilla Pudding, (recipe p. 230.) cooked	2 cups	3 qt.
Coffee Cream	1/2 cup	3 cups
Dark Rum *or* Rum Extract	to taste	to taste

METHOD

1. Combine flour, sugar, milk powder, salt, baking powder, and shortening.
2. Slowly add the water, eggs, vanilla, and egg shade. Pour into greased 16- by 24-inch sheet pans. (Single cakes can be baked round and layered in 3 spring-form pans.) Bake in preheated oven at 400°F. for 35 minutes. Cool. Cut cake in sheet pan into four strips.
3. Spread each layer with Cinnamon-Sugar Icing made by combining icing ingredients with a beater. Arrange in aluminum foil-lined mold as follows: cake, whipped ice cream, cake, whipped ice cream, cake. Freeze.
4. When cakes are firm, unmold and frost tops and sides with Cinnamon-Sugar Icing, then pat mixture of macaroon crumbs and ground pecans into frosting. Refreeze. Serve with Eggnog Sauce.
5. Mix all icing ingredients together with wire beater.
6. Whip ice cream to consistency of soft ice cream; use flat beater and start slowly.
7. Combine all Eggnog Sauce ingredients to sauce-like consistency and desired flavor.

RAISIN PUMPKIN MUFFINS

(A spicy batter than can be refrigerated and baked as needed)

YIELD:	2 DOZEN	24 DOZEN
INGREDIENTS		
Cake Flour	3-1/2 cups	9 lb.
Granulated Sugar	5 cups	3-3/4 lb.
Baking Powder	1-1/2 tsp.	3 oz.
Salt	1 tsp.	2 oz.
Cinnamon	1/2 tsp.	1 oz.
Nutmeg	1/2 tsp.	1 oz.
Shortening, melted	3 tbsp.	2-1/4 cups
Egg	1	2-1/4 cups
Milk	1/2 cup	3 qt.
Pumpkin, Canned	1/3 cup	5 lb., 8 oz.
Raisins	1 cup	3 lb.

METHOD

1. Mix together cake flour, sugar, baking powder, salt, cinnamon, and nutmeg with a paddle beater.
2. While beating, add the melted shortening.
3. Combine the egg, milk, pumpkin, raisins, and add to the above mixture.
4. Bake in greased muffin pans in oven at 400°F. for 20 to 25 minutes.

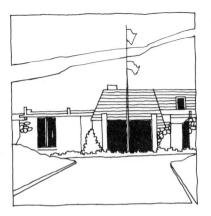

Atlanta Athletic Club

Beverly Hills Tennis Club

Beverly Hills, California

One member called it "an oasis in Beverly Hills." But the Beverly Hills Tennis Club is approached on bicycle, not camelback, as early as 8 a.m. by many of the 163 members who come to pay court to the body beautiful.

With a large number of doctors, a few movie industry personalities, and the normal sprinkling of health food enthusiasts, the membership has to be one of the most diet-conscious in clubdom.

HORSERADISH BEET SALAD

(Lively to the tongue and lovely to the eye)

YIELD:	6 PORTIONS	24 PORTIONS

INGREDIENTS

			METHOD
Beets, cooked, cut julienne	2 cups	8 cups	1. Combine beets with sour cream which has been seasoned to taste with horseradish, salt, and cayenne pepper.
Sour Cream	1/2 cup	2 cups	2. Serve garnished with chopped chives or scallions.
Horseradish	1 tsp.	4 tsp.	
Salt	1/2 tsp.	2 tsp.	
Cayenne Pepper	dash	1/8 tsp.	
Chives *or* Scallions, chopped	1 tbsp.	1/4 cup	

CORNED BEEF AND TONGUE LOAF

(A low-cost loaf that looks and tastes like headcheese)

YIELD:	2-1/2 POUNDS	12 POUNDS

INGREDIENTS

			METHOD
Tongue, cooked, peeled	1 lb.	6 lb.	1. Cut tongue and corned beef into 1/2-inch dice.
Corned Beef, cooked	1 lb.	5 lb.	2. Add dill pickles, green olives, pimiento, carrots, vinegar, and pepper.
Dill Pickles, Large, diced	2	10	3. Cook down and then add gelatine to thicken mixture.
Stuffed Green Olives, drained	1/4 cup	1 No. 2 can	4. Pour into loaf pans and bake. Turn out and serve in 1/4-inch slices.
Pimiento, drained, diced	1/4 cup	2 3-oz. cans	
Carrots, Large, diced, cooked	1	5	
Wine Vinegar	to taste	to taste	
Black Pepper, freshly ground	to taste	to taste	
Gelatine, Unflavored	2 tbsp.	1/4 lb.	

TENNIS CLUB ANTIPASTO ★

(A low-calorie appetizer assortment)

YIELD:	5 to 10 PORTIONS	30 to 40 PORTIONS
INGREDIENTS		
Olive Oil	1/4 cup	1 cup
Garlic, peeled and crushed or chopped	1/2 clove	2 cloves
Green Beans	2 oz.	1/4 lb.
Mushrooms	1/2 lb.	2 lb.
Onion, chopped	1 small	2 large
Green Pepper, cut in strips	1	4
Carrots, cut in strips	1-1/2	6
Zucchini, cut in strips	1-1/2	6
Cauliflower, broken into flowerlets	1/4 head	1 head
Celery, cut in strips	1-1/2 ribs	6 ribs
Tomato Sauce	1/2 cup	1 No. 2 can
Catsup	1/2 cup	1 14-oz. bottle
Salt	to taste	to taste
Pepper	to taste	to taste
Oregano	to taste	to taste
Sweet Basil	to taste	to taste
Tuna	1 7-oz. can	3 7-oz. cans
Sardines	1 can	3 cans
Ripe Olives	1/2 cup	1-1/2 cups
Green Olives	1/2 cup	1-1/2 cups

METHOD

1. Cook all except last 4 ingredients together until vegetables are tender but still crisp.
2. Before serving, garnish with tuna, sardines, and olives.

★ See picture, facing page.

TENNIS CLUB ANTIPASTO

Olive
Administrative
Committee

CELERY ROOT AND ANCHOVY ROLLS ★

(A seldom-used vegetable makes a prestigious salad or appetizer)

YIELD:	6 PORTIONS	24 PORTIONS
INGREDIENTS		
Celery Root	1/4 lb.	1 lb.
Vinaigrette Dressing (recipe p. 236)	1/4 cup	1 cup
Rolled Anchovy Fillets	1/2 oz.	2 oz.

METHOD

1. Cook celery root in lightly salted water; cool in the water.
2. Peel and slice in 1/4-inch slices.
3. Dip into Vinaigrette Dressing and arrange on a platter or salad plates.
4. Garnish with rolled anchovy fillets.

STUFFED BONELESS CHICKEN

(Boned chicken stuffed with tongue, more chicken, pistachio nuts, and hard-cooked eggs)

YIELD:	8 PORTIONS	24 PORTIONS
INGREDIENTS		
Raw Chicken, finely ground	4 lb.	12 lb.
Onion, chopped, sauteed	1	3
Egg Bread, torn	1 loaf (1 lb.)	3 loaves (1 lb. each)
Milk	2 cups	6 cups
Salt	1 tsp.	1 tbsp.
White Pepper	1/4 tsp.	1 tsp.
Sherry	1/2 cup	1-1/2 cups
Heavy Cream	1/2 cup	1-1/2 cups
Eggs	3	9
Tongue, cooked, sliced	1 lb.	3 lb.
Eggs, hard-cooked, chopped	2	6
Pistachio Nuts	1/4 cup	3/4 cup
Chicken, boned	2 to 3 lb.	6 to 9 lb.
Chicken Broth	2 cups	6 cups
Chaudfroid Sauce (recipe, p. 224)		

METHOD

1. Combine ground raw chicken with sauteed onion, bread which has been soaked in milk, salt, pepper, and sherry. Grind this mixture together and thin with combined cream and eggs.
2. Use mixture, together with strips of tongue, whole peeled hard-cooked eggs, and whole pistachio nuts, to line boned chicken.
3. Roll, wrap in cheesecloth, and tie securely.
4. Poach in chicken broth and cool.
5. Coat with chaudfroid and decorate as you like.

★ See picture, facing page.

CELERY ROOT AND ANCHOVY ROLLS

COLD ROULADE OF BEEF ★

(An excellent buffet item, popular with men for cocktail parties)

YIELD:	40 SLICES	160 SLICES

INGREDIENTS		
Top Round of Beef, thinly sliced	1 lb.	4 lb.
Black Pepper, freshly ground	to taste	to taste
Onion, very thinly sliced	1 small	1 large
Bacon Slices	8	32
Dill Pickles, cut in thin strips	2	8
Beef Aspic (recipe, p. 233)	as needed	as needed

METHOD

1. Pound beef and season with pepper. Cover with onion and slices of bacon. Arrange pickle strips along 1 edge and roll ment tightly so that pickle will be in the center.
2. Place on greased pan and braise in oven at 350°F. for 30 minutes.
3. Cool, slice, and coat with aspic. When aspic has set, arrange roulades on a platter for service. Keep cool until serving time.

PINEAPPLE-CARROT SOUR CREAM SALAD ★ ★

(A refreshing, attractive salad or appetizer with special appeal for women)

YIELD:	6 PORTIONS	24 PORTIONS

INGREDIENTS		
Carrots, peeled, grated	4	16
Pineapple, Crushed, drained	2-1/2 cups	10 cups
Sour Cream	1 cup	1 qt.
Fresh Lime Juice	1/4 cup	1 cup
Coconut, Shredded	1/2 cup	2 cups
Maraschino Cherries, Red or Green (optional)	6	24

METHOD

1. Serve carrots and pineapple with sour cream which has been seasoned with lime juice.
2. Garnish with coconut and cherries. Serve on lettuce, if desired.

★   See picture, facing page.
★ ★   See picture, page 20.

COLD ROULADE OF BEEF

Pickle
Packers
International

PINEAPPLE-CARROT SOUR CREAM SALAD

Castle and
Cooke Foods,
Inc.

Bohemian Club

San Francisco, California

There's no deadwood in the redwoods . . . if one is to judge by the 3,000-acre area called Bohemian Grove, where, each July, 1,800 lively members of San Francisco's Bohemian Club exercise their talents among the shady sequoia trees.

The group also owns and operates in San Francisco proper a club with 54 sleeping rooms, a number of dining rooms, and a professionally equipped theatre. Here members stage their own productions—sometimes even opera—do their own lighting, costumes, music, et al.

The theatrical Bohemians are not so bohemian as to be disinterested in their weight. Diet items are popular on the menu, and they include one seldom seen elsewhere; broiled lamb kidney is featured on a rotating basis with breast of turkey, broiled ground beef, and lean roast beef.

Dominoes is very popular in San Francisco, and the Bohemian Club is one of the few with a domino room at the ready, with 50 tables for play and small side tables nearby for food and drink.

SANTA BARBARA FIGS

(Fresh figs with thinly sliced ham cornets filled with seasoned cheese)

YIELD:	6 PORTIONS	24 PORTIONS
INGREDIENTS		
Fresh Figs	9	36
Gervais Cheese		
or		
Cream Cheese	3 oz.	12 oz.
Salt	to taste	to taste
Pepper	to taste	to taste
Prosciutto		
or		
Westphalian Ham	6 slices	24 slices

METHOD
1. Cut figs in half.
2. Scoop out part of the pulp and fill each cavity with gervais cheese or cream cheese, lightly seasoned with salt and pepper.
3. Top with prosciutto or Westphalian ham cornets.
4. On service platter, alternate green and blue figs.

ALSATIAN HUNTER'S LUNCH

(Three flavorful meats served with sauerkraut and split peas)

YIELD:	1 PORTION	24 PORTIONS
INGREDIENTS		
Sauerkraut	3/4 cup	18 cups
Smoked Pork Loin, sliced	1 slice	24 slices
Swiss Sausage (bratwurst)	1	24
Smoked Bacon, boiled, sliced	1 slice	24 slices
Parsley Potatoes	2	48
Split Peas, pureed	1/3 cup	8 cups
Onion, diced, sauteed	1/2	12

METHOD
1. Start with a platter of sauerkraut. Top sauerkraut with a slice of smoked pork loin, a Swiss sausage (bratwurst), a slice of boiled smoked bacon, and parsley potatoes.
2. Garnish with puree of peas topped with sauteed diced onion.

CHICKEN SAUTE A LA MORNE DE GUADELOUPE

(An island favorite flavored with white wine and coconut milk and garnished with sauteed bananas and toasted, crushed peanuts)

YIELD:	4 PORTIONS	24 PORTIONS
INGREDIENTS		
Spring Chicken	1	6
Lemon Juice	1 tbsp.	1/3 cup
Salt	1/2 tsp.	1 tbsp.
Pepper	1/8 tsp.	3/4 tsp.
Butter	1/4 cup	1-1/2 cup
Green Onions, sliced	2	12
Ham, diced	1/4 cup	1-1/2 cup
White Wine	1/2 cup	3 cups
Coconut Milk	1/2 cup	3 cups
Cornstarch (optional)	1 tsp.	2 tbsp.

METHOD

1. Cut spring chicken into quarters and bone in usual manner. Sprinkle chicken with lemon juice, salt, and pepper. Let set about 2 hours. Saute chicken in butter until browned lightly and evenly on all sides. Remove from pan.
2. To saute pan, add sliced green onions and diced ham. When onions are sauteed to point of transparency, add 1/2 white wine and 1/2 coconut milk.
3. Return chicken to pan and simmer until it is tender.
4. Thicken slightly with cornstarch, if desired.
5. At the Bohemian Club this is served with bananas which have been sauteed in butter and rolled in toasted, crushed peanuts; glazed sweet potatoes or ducesse potatoes and fried zucchini.

Bohemian Club

The Cleveland Yachting Club

Cleveland, Ohio

The Cleveland Yachting Club is located on an island right where the Rocky River empties into Lake Erie. In 1913, a year before the first clubhouse was floated in on 3 barges (pulled by a single tug), a county road bridge was built to link the island to the mainland.

The island has had a colorful history, including a stint during prohibition when rum runners used the lagoon in their illegal operations.

A striking feature of the entrance lobby of the new clubhouse is a ship's wheel from one of the old Great Lakes freighters. When the ship was finally taken out of commission, the family presented the wheel to the club.

Out front, resting in a bed of flowers, there is an anchor dating back to sailing ship days. All things are pleasantly nautical here . . . there seems to be a bit of Walter Mitty in all of us.

ROAST TENDERLOIN OF BEEF CLEVELAND YACHT CLUB STYLE
(Tender tenderloin marinated in Burgundy then roasted with oregano, shallots, and bacon)

YIELD:	6 PORTIONS	24 PORTIONS
INGREDIENTS		
Burgundy	2 cups	8
Wine Vinegar	2 tsp.	3 tbsp.
Olive Oil	1 tsp.	1 tbsp.
Beef Tenderloin	3 lb.	12 lb.
Salt	to taste	to taste
Pepper	to taste	to taste
Oregano	to taste	to taste
Shallots, chopped	as needed	as needed
Bacon	6 slices	24 slices
Roux (recipe, p. 233)	as needed	as needed

METHOD

1. Combine half of the Burgundy with vinegar and olive oil to make a marinade. Pour over tenderloin and set in cooler overnight.
2. Drain well. Sprinkle with seasonings and chopped shallots. Lay bacon slices on top and roast to desired finish. (15 minutes at 400°F. will be rare.)
3. Strain juice; add remaining half of the Burgundy; thicken with a roux. Season to taste; simmer until served. Place tenderloin slices on top of the gravy.

WET HEN CREPES
(Wet hens are the female first mates at the Cleveland Yachting Club where these chicken crepes with mushrooms and Parmesan cheese are a flag-flying favorite)

YIELD:	6 PORTIONS	24 PORTIONS
INGREDIENTS		
Stewing Chicken	6 to 8 lb.	24 lb.
Celery	1 rib	4 ribs
Bay Leaf	1	4
Shallots	4	16
Carrot, sliced	1	4
Mushrooms, sliced	2 cups	2 qt.
Sweet Basil	1/2 tsp.	2 tsp.
Crepes, large	6	24
Parmesan Cheese, grated	1 tbsp.	1/4 cup
Paprika	to garnish	to garnish

METHOD

1. Boil chicken with celery, bay leaf, shallots, and carrot. When fowl is tender remove from stock; bone and dice.
2. Make Poulet Sauce (recipe, page 227) from the stock, adding mushrooms and basil. Fold chicken into sauce.
3. Spoon 1 cup of chicken mixture onto each crepe. Lay out on baking dish and cover with Poulet Sauce. Sprinkle with grated cheese and a bit of paprika for color.
4. Bake in oven at 375°F. for 15 minutes. If necessary, slip under broiler for additional browning.

CLAMS ROCKY RIVER

(Poached clams in a Brandy-Sherry Sauce, served with crisp toast points)

YIELD:	2 PORTIONS	24 PORTIONS
INGREDIENTS		
Clams, Medium-sized	2 doz.	48 doz.
Shallots, finely chopped	2	24
Butter	4 tsp.	1/2 lb.
Dry Sherry	1/4 cup	3 cups
Brandy	1 tbsp.	3/4 cup
Salt	to taste	to taste
Pepper	to taste	to taste
Nutmeg	to taste	to taste
Cream	1 cup	3 qt.
Egg Yolks	3	36
Butter	1 tsp.	8 oz.

METHOD

1. Poach clams in their own juice, adding only as much water as necessary. When clams are firm to the touch, drain and set aside.
2. Saute shallots in butter until soft, but not brown.
3. Add clams, sherry, brandy, seasonings, and cream.
4. Thicken sauce with beaten egg yolks; add second amount of butter.
5. Serve with toast points.

SHRIMP A LA MARIO

(Cheese, garlic, and mustard flavor sauteed shrimp with sherry; lemon makes a last minute contribution)

YIELD:	6 PORTIONS	24 PORTIONS
INGREDIENTS		
Shrimp, uncooked, shelled	3 lb.	10 lb.
Egg Wash*	1 egg	4 eggs
Bread Crumbs, dried	2 cups	20 oz. (2 qt.)
Romano Cheese, grated	1/2 cup	2 cups
Garlic Concentrate	1 tsp.	4 tsp.
Dry Mustard	1 tsp.	4 tsp.
Salt	to taste	to taste
White Pepper	to taste	to taste
Butter	1/2 cup	2 cups
Dry Sherry	1 cup	32 oz. (1 qt.)
Lemon, juice of	1	4

METHOD

1. Dip raw shrimp in egg wash, then in mixture of bread crumbs, cheese, garlic, mustard, salt, and pepper.
2. Saute in butter until golden.
3. At the last minute add wine and lemon juice.
4. Serve on a hot platter with pan juices poured over all.

*Egg Wash is prepared by adding 1 tbsp. cold water per egg and beating to blend.

CHEESE-SPINACH SOUFFLE

(A souffle that can be mixed ahead and held 30 minutes before it goes to the oven)

YIELD: **6 PORTIONS**

INGREDIENTS		METHOD
Eggs	6	1. Beat eggs well; add remaining ingredients except Parmesan; stir well.
Cheddar Cheese	3 cups	
Spinach, cooked, chopped	1 cup	2. Carefully butter individual souffle cups and sprinkle with Parmesan cheese; fill 3/4 full with egg mixture.
Bread Crumbs, soft	2 cups	
Dry Mustard	1 tbsp.	
Chicken Base	1 tsp.	3. Set cups in 1/2 inch of water in baking pan.
Parsley, chopped	2 tsp.	4. Bake in oven at 375°F. for 45 minutes. Serve immediately with a Mushroom Sauce (recipe, p. 229).
Chives, chopped	2 tsp.	
Parmesan Cheese, grated	as needed	

Note   Unbaked souffles can be held in a pan of warm, but not simmering, water for as long as 30 minutes, which allows baking to order.

The Cleveland Yachting Club

Concordia-Argonaut Club

San Francisco, California

Have you ever heard of a Hangtown Fry? It is a flat omelet with strips of bacon crossed in the pan and fresh oysters scattered like gold nuggets (and costing almost as much these days) around the cross. Any gold field varmint about to be executed in San Francisco was served Hangtown Fry as his last meal . . . perhaps to give him strength as he changed from gold-seeker to fire-feeder.

And did you know that those old covered wagons that pop across the television screen now and then were known as argonauts? The name was derived by analogy from the Argo, which Jason sailed in quest of the Golden Fleece. A very apt name considering that most of the covered wagons were headed for the California gold fields.

Many of the members of San Francisco's Concordia-Argonaut Club trace their ancestry back to pioneers who made that long, hard trek in argonauts. Few acknowledge Hangtown Fryers on the family tree, but the club has placed a replica of an argonaut over the mantle of the huge, stone fireplace in the main lounge, and Hangtown Fry is often on the menu.

The Concordia part of the club's name stems from a Concordia Society established in 1864. The name with its connotation of peace was taken from "Die Glocke," a poem by Schiller, which was popular about that time.

PRAWNS ANTOINETTE

(Shrimp or mussels may be substituted for prawns)

YIELD:	6 PORTIONS	24 PORTIONS	METHOD
INGREDIENTS			1. Combine all ingredients.
Mayonnaise	1 cup	4 cups	2. Marinate overnight. Serve on lettuce leaves.
Salad Oil	1/4 cup	1 cup	
Chili Sauce	3 tbsp.	3/4 cup	
Celery Seed	1 tsp.	1 tbsp. plus 1 tsp.	
Garlic, minced	1 clove	4 cloves	
Onion, Medium sized, chopped	1/2	2	
Celery Rib with leaves, chopped	1 rib	4 ribs	
Dill, chopped	1 sprig	4 sprigs	
Prawns, cooked, shelled, deveined	2 lb.	8 lb.	

PINK TURKEY SLAW

(A simply made buffet money-maker)

YIELD:	5 PORTIONS	20 PORTIONS	METHOD
INGREDIENTS			1. Combine first four ingredients; toss with shredded cabbage.
Mayonnaise	1/2 cup	2 cups	2. Garnish with turkey just before serving.
Catsup	1/3 cup	1-1/3 cups	
Salt	1/8 tsp.	1/2 tsp.	
Pepper, freshly ground	1/8 tsp.	1/2 tsp.	
Cabbage, finely shredded	1/2 head	2 heads	
Turkey Breast, julienne	1 cup	1/4 lb.	

RAW CELERY ROOT SALAD
(Crisp, white and tart)

YIELD:	5 PORTIONS	20 PORTIONS
INGREDIENTS		
Celery Roots, peeled	3	12
Salt	1/2 tbsp.	2 tbsp.
White Pepper, ground	1/2 tsp.	2 tsp.
Lemon, juice of	1	4
Mayonnaise	1-1/2 cups	6 cups
Parsley, chopped	to garnish	to garnish

METHOD
1. Slice celery roots 1/4 inch thick and cut in julienne slices.
2. Combine remaining ingredients except parsley; stir together with strips of celery root.
3. Garnish with chopped parsley when serving.

HANGTOWN FRY
(Deep-fried oysters framed in bacon topped with eggs)

YIELD:	1 SERVING
INGREDIENTS	
Clarified Butter	as needed
Bacon, crisp	2 slices
Oysters, breaded, deep-fried	3
Eggs, beaten	2

METHOD
1. Put clarified butter in a 7-inch black, cast-iron fry pan.
2. Add slices of bacon to form a cross and place oysters between the slices.
3. Add eggs and cook slowly like a flat omelet.
4. Serve soft.

SWEET AND SOUR SALMON
(A sweet-sour Madeira Sauce with plump raisins beautifully accents poached salmon steak)

YIELD:	5 PORTIONS	20 PORTIONS
INGREDIENTS		
Madeira Sauce, Brown (recipe p. 228)	1 cup	1 qt.
Raisins	3 tbsp.	5 oz.
White Wine Vinegar	1/4 cup	1 cup
Brown Sugar	2 tbsp.	1/4 lb.
Salmon Steaks, poached	5	20
Cookie Crumbs	1/4 cup	1 cup

METHOD
1. Use Madeira Sauce as a base.
2. Cook the raisins in water until tender. Drain and add to the sauce together with vinegar and brown sugar.
3. Stir and cook 15 minutes.
4. Ladle sauce over salmon steaks and sprinkle cookie crumbs on top.

Cosmos Club

Washington, D. C.

Although the hand of history no longer rests directly on the walls of Washington's famed Cosmos Club since it moved to new quarters in the nation's capital, there does remain the imperishable imprint of the club's unofficial patron—Dolly Madison.

Until 1952 a part of the club's home was a yellow stucco, white-shuttered residence which had once been the home of the controversial Dolly. Then the government, more concerned with the present than the past, embarked on an expansion program and earmarked the Madison-Cosmos home for demolition.

Before the wrecker's steel ball could start swinging, another notable first lady made her presence felt. Jacqueline Kennedy is credited with saving the structure, and it now provides judges' chambers for the new federal court building being erected behind it.

With the U. S. government's $1 million payment (a copy of the check is on display in the new building), the Cosmos Club purchased a beautiful French Renaissance mansion elsewhere in Washington. In homage to their lady, Dolly, the members had the walls above the wainscoting in a center room painted as though one were on the street near the old home, looking about the neighborhood as it was in Dolly's day.

CHICKEN AND AVOCADO SOUP

(A "hot" chicken soup garnished with diced avocado and breast of chicken)

YIELD:	6 PORTIONS	24 PORTIONS
INGREDIENTS		
Chicken	1/2 lb.	2 lb.
Chicken Broth	1 qt.	1 gal.
Carrot	1/2	2
Celery	1/2 rib	2 ribs
Leek	1/2	2
Onion	1/2	2
Chicken Bouillon	1 cube	1 tsp.
Avocado,* diced		
or balled	1	4
Salt	to taste	to taste
Pepper	to taste	to taste
Liquid Hot Pepper		
Seasoning	to taste	to taste

METHOD

1. Cook chicken in the usual manner in chicken broth or water with carrot, celery, leek, and onion until done. If cooked in water, add chicken bouillon for extra strength.
2. Bone and skin chicken, reserving breast for garnish.
3. Strain broth, using vegetables and chicken legs for chicken stew. Add salt, pepper, and liquid hot pepper seasoning.
4. Garnish soup with diced avocado and diced breast of chicken.

*When prepared ahead, coat well with lemon juice to prevent discoloration.

Cosmos Club

HERB-FRIED CHICKEN

(A flavorful, crisp, golden crust makes this fried chicken unique)

YIELD:	6 PORTIONS	24 PORTIONS
INGREDIENTS		
Salt	1 tsp.	4 tsp.
Pepper	1/4 tsp.	1 tsp.
Thyme	1/4 tsp.	1 tsp.
Marjoram	1/4 tsp.	1 tsp.
Shallots, chopped	1 tbsp.	1/4 cup
Parsley, chopped	1 tbsp.	1/4 cup
Bread Crumbs	2 cups	8 cups
or		
Flour	1/2 cup	2 cups
Frying Chicken, disjointed	2 to 2-1/2 lb.	8 to 10 lb.
Half-and-Half		
or		
Milk	1 cup	1 qt.
Maple Syrup	1 tsp.	4 tsp.
Ginger	1/4 tsp.	1 tsp.
Eggs, beaten	2	8
Peanut Oil	as needed	as needed

METHOD

1. Combine seasonings, shallots, and parsley with bread crumbs or flour.
2. Dip chicken pieces in mixture of milk, maple syrup, ginger, and eggs. Drain off excess moisture.
3. Roll in bread crumbs or flour with seasonings.
4. Brown chicken pieces evenly in peanut oil (10 to 15 minutes). Remove chicken from skillet; place on sheet pan and sprinkle with remaining crumbs and seasoning; brush with melted butter. Bake in oven at 375°F. for 15 to 20 minutes, or until done.

PETITE POT DE CREME A LA MARGOT ★

(A light and lovely dessert flavored with chocolate, almond, and pistachio)

YIELD:	10 PORTIONS	60 PORTIONS
INGREDIENTS		
Coffee Cream	2/3 cup	1 qt.
Bitter Chocolate, grated	1/3 oz.	2 oz.
Granulated Sugar	1/2 cup	1-1/2 lb.
Gelatine, Unflavored	1 tbsp.	2 oz.
Filbert Ice Cream	2/3 cup	1 qt.
or		
Almond Paste	2-2/3 oz.	1 lb.
Heavy Cream, whipped	2/3 cup	1 qt.
Pistachio Nuts, finely chopped	2 tbsp. (1 oz.)	4 oz.
Cream, whipped	1/3 cup	1 pt.
Maraschino Cherries, well-drained	10	60

METHOD

1. Heat cream and chocolate together to scalding; add sugar and gelatine; remove from heat. Do not allow to boil.
2. Stir in ice cream or almond paste, melting it in the hot mixture. Then stir over ice until mixture begins to jell.
3. Fold in whipped cream and nuts.
4. Fill 3-ounce dishes and refrigerate. Garnish each with a rosette of whipped cream and a stemmed red maraschino cherry.

★ See picture, facing page.

PETITE POT DE CREME A LA MARGOT

National Cherry
Growers and
Industries Foun-
dation

Dallas Country Club

Dallas, Texas

The oldest club in Dallas, established in 1896, the Dallas Country Club is now near the heart of the city. It is a city club with an 18-hole golf course and a swimming pool!

One of the most popular events at the club is the monthly "shrimp peel." Its popularity is credited to the fact that even the most sophisticated of sophisticates likes the informality of a dinner where one picks hot shrimp from a pot and peels them by hand.

The shrimp are first cooked in beer (see recipe, page 39) and then presented in an old-fashioned iron laundry pot placed on a small, round table in the middle of the dining room. Canned heat makes a fire beneath the pot and keeps the liquor from the cooked shrimp steaming in the bottom of the pot. The shrimp actually rest on a small grate above the liquid.

Another old Texas favorite, popular at the club, is black-eyed peas. In Texas they treat black-eyed peas as Yankees treat their navy beans, with hot pepper sauce taking the role of vinegar. The hot sauce at the Dallas Country Club comes in three degrees—hot, hotter, and hottest. The fire-eating members reportedly "just drink" the very hottest. The peas are cooked with onion, chopped fine enough to disappear, and bacon is added, so finely cut that it leaves only its flavor behind. A few hours of simmering and the peas are ready for the fiery sauce.

DALLAS COUNTRY CLUB GUMBO

(Real old-fashioned seafood soup—thick and hearty)

YIELD:	10 PORTIONS	100 PORTIONS
INGREDIENTS		
Celery, medium-dice	1 rib	3 lb.
Bell Pepper, medium-dice	1/2	2-1/2 lb.
Onion, 1-inch dice	1	5 lb.
Oil	as needed	as needed
Rosemary	1/4 tsp.	1 tbsp.
Thyme	1/2 tsp	2 tbsp.
Gumbo File	1 tsp	4 level cook spoons*
Flavor Enhancer	1/2 tsp.	2 level cook spoons
Salt	1/2 tsp.	2 level cook spoons
Black Pepper, finely ground	pinch	1/2 level cook spoon
Fish Stock	2-1/2 qt.	6 gal.
Roux**		
Okra	1/3 lb.	3 lb.
Tomato Paste	4 tsp.	6 oz.
Tomatoes, Canned	3/4 cup	1/2 gal.
Rotel Tomatoes with Peppers	1/4 can	2 cans
Flaked Seafoods***	as preferred	as preferred
Rice, cooked	as needed	as needed

METHOD

1. Braise first 3 ingredients in oil; add herbs and seasonings.
2. Stir in stock and bring to a boil. Add remaining ingredients, except seafood, rice, and roux; simmer for 40 minutes.
3. Thicken with roux to the consistency of a heavy cream soup and continue to simmer 20 minutes.
4. Add seafood and rice; heat through and serve.

*"Cook spoon" measure refers to the large spoon used for stirring in a restaurant kitchen.

**A roux is made by melting butter and mixing in an equal amount of flour.

***The Dallas Country Club suggests haddock, cod, whitefish, shrimp, and bone meat from red snapper.

SWEETBREADS WITH BURGUNDY SAUCE
(Delicate sweetbreads served in a wine sauce on noodles)

YIELD:	3 to 4 PORTIONS	24 PORTIONS
INGREDIENTS		
Sweetbreads	1 lb.	6 lb.
Salt	2 tbsp.	3/4 cup
Vinegar	2 tbsp.	3/4 cup
Salt	1/2 tsp.	1 tbsp.
Bay Leaf	1	6
Lemon, juice and pulp of	1/2	3
Onion, diced	1	6
Celery, chunked	1 rib	6 ribs
Flour	as needed	as needed
Salt	as needed	as needed
Pepper	as needed	as needed
Paprika	as needed	as needed
Cooking Oil	as needed	as needed
SAUCE		
Broth from Sweetbreads		
Cornstarch *or* Flour	as needed	as needed
Burgundy	1 cup	6 cups
Noodles, cooked, buttered	3 cups	18 cups

METHOD

1. Soak sweetbreads for about 5 minutes in water to which the 2 tbsp. salt and vinegar have been added. Peel sweetbreads and cook for 20 minutes in water to which you have added 1/2 tsp. salt, bay leaf, lemon (squeeze, then add both juice and peel to the water), onion, and celery. Drain and chill, saving broth.

2. Slice cold sweetbreads 1/4 to 3/8 inch thick. Dredge in flour to which salt, pepper, and paprika have been added. Brown in a small amount of oil.

3. To make sauce, thicken broth to medium consistency (2 tbsp. flour per cup of liquid). Reduce Burgundy to half and add to the sauce. Simmer to desired thickness and pour over sweetbreads. Bake in oven at 350° F. for 15 to 20 minutes.

4. Serve on buttered noodles.

SHRIMP PEEL

(You peel the flavorful shrimp at the table)

YIELD:	20 PORTIONS	425 to 450 PORTIONS
INGREDIENTS		
Celery, chopped	1/2 rib	1 stalk
Onion, small, peeled, quartered	1	6
Garlic, peeled	1 clove	1 pod
Lemon, quartered	1/2	8
Ice Cream Salt	3 tbsp.	4 cups
Paprika	1-1/2 tbsp.	2 cups
Chili Powder	1-1/2 tbsp.	2 cups
Shrimp Boil Spice* *or* Pickling Spice	1 tsp.	1/2 cup
Beer	1-1/2 cups	2 gal.
Shrimp	10 lb.	208 lb.

METHOD

1. Simmer vegetables, lemon, and seasonings in water to cover shrimp. Add beer and shrimp. Return to boiling and simmer for 5 minutes, or until shrimp are barely cooked. Do not overcook.

*Shrimp Boil is a commercially available seasoning for boiling seafood.

SAUCE FOR SHRIMP PEEL

YIELD:	20 PORTIONS	425 to 450 PORTIONS
INGREDIENTS		
Celery, diced	1/2 rib	1 stalk
Onion, diced	1/2	4 large
Green Pepper, diced	1/2	8
Garlic, peeled and pressed	2 cloves	2 pods
Olive Oil	1/2 cup	3 qt.
Chili Powder	2-1/2 tsp.	1 cup
Paprika	2-1/2 tsp.	1 cup
Shrimp Boil Spices	1-1/4 tsp.	1/2 cup
Burgundy	1/2 cup	1/2 gal.

METHOD

1. Saute vegetables and garlic in oil.
2. Add seasonings and wine.
3. Do not reduce mixture.

ELOISE WALKER'S FAMOUS HUSH PUPPIES ★
(Serve with any kind of fish or alone as an hors d'oeuvre)

YIELD:	16 PORTIONS	160 PORTIONS
INGREDIENTS		
White Corn Meal	1/2 lb.	5 lb.
White Onion, Medium-Sized, finely chopped	1/3	3
Chives *or* Young Scallion Tops (optional)	1 tbsp.	1/2 cup
Bacon, fried, crumbled	2 tbsp.	1 cup
Granulated Sugar	1 tbsp.	1 cup
Baking Powder	2 tsp.	3 oz.
Salt	1/2 tsp.	1 oz.
Vegetable Oil	1/4 cup	2-1/2 cups
Water	2 cups	5 qt.
Peanut Oil, to deep fry	as needed	as needed

METHOD

1. Combine first 7 ingredients.
2. Rub in the vegetable oil.
3. Bring water to a hard boil and mix about two-thirds of it into the hush puppies.
4. Gradually add boiling water to a consistency that can be rolled for frying.
5. Shape into 2-1/2- by 1-inch cylinders.
6. Freeze for future use, or fry in deep fat at 360°F. immediately.

★ See picture, facing page.

ELOISE WALKER'S FAMOUS HUSH PUPPIES

Peanut
Associates,
Inc.

The Denver Club

Denver, Colorado

The Denver Club was born in 1880, and, like many downtown clubs, its early youth was spent in rented space on the second floor of an old hotel. It moved from there to an impressive stone bastion on 17th Street (which is akin to New York's Wall Street). Today the club owns the top 4 floors of a skyscraper erected on the site of the former clubhouse.

Wild game is plentiful and popular in the Denver area, and, though buffalo is no longer considered wild game (the club's supply is acquired from Bison Pete's Buffalo Farm in Wyoming), the noble beast has an honored spot on the menu. The meat is prepared by roasting the round and serving it as you would beef. The parts of the buffalo which are not roasted are ground to be served as Buffalo Burgers with a barbecue sauce.

Elk is roasted, too, but antelope is cut into steaks, which are dipped in flour and then sauteed. Unused elk meat goes into elk sausage, and mincemeat is made from venison. The mincemeat is used both for pies and for cookies. (See recipe, page 46.)

Game dumplings are another unusual item sometimes served at the club. The dumplings are a combination of ground pheasant and venison, together with egg yolks, half-and-half, mushrooms, truffle peelings, pimiento, seasonings, Pernod, and Cognac. The mixture is shaped into small dumplings, the size of 25-cent pieces and simmered in hot water or Pheasant Soup.

Pheasant Soup is a brew of pheasant stock, flavored with root vegetables and pickling spice, strained and thickened with a beurre manie made from butter and flour. Some red wine and cream are added.

HOT BLOODY MARY SOUP

(An add-your-own-gin soup for those who love the flavor of Bloody Marys)

YIELD:	8 PORTIONS	32 PORTIONS
INGREDIENTS		
Bay Leaf	1/3	1
Garlic	1/8 tsp.	1/2 tsp.
Granulated Sugar	1/8 tsp.	1/2 tsp.
Liquid Hot Pepper Seasoning	1 drop	4 drops
Worcestershire Sauce	1 drop	4 drops
Tomato Beverage Mix	1/2 can (6 oz. can)	2 cans (6 oz. can)
Tomato Juice	1/4 can (14 oz. can)	1 can 14 oz. can)
Consomme Madrilene	1/2 can (13 oz. can)	2 cans (13 oz. can)
Tomato, diced, peeled	1/2	2
Green Pepper, diced	1/4	1
Breast of Chicken *or* Turkey, diced	1/4 cup	1 cup
Salt	to taste	to taste
Pepper	to taste	to taste
Gin	to taste	to taste

METHOD

1. Combine all ingredients except gin and heat.
2. Serve with gin on the side and let diners add it to taste.

BARBECUED LAMB SHANKS WITH VERMOUTH ★

(Lamb, Pork, or Poultry take on added interest from this marinade)

YIELD:	6 PORTIONS	24 PORTIONS
INGREDIENTS		
Lamb, Pork, *or* Poultry Shanks	6	24
Dry Vermouth	1 cup	4 cups
Oil	1 cup	4 cups
Lemon Juice	1-1/2 tsp.	2 tbsp.
Shallots, chopped *or*	3	12
Onion, Medium-Sized	1	4
Garlic, minced	2 cloves	8 cloves
Fresh Tarragon, chopped *or*	1 tsp.	2 tsp.
Dried Tarragon	1/2 tsp.	2 tsp.
Fresh Basil, chopped *or*	1 tsp.	4 tsp.
Dried Basil	1/2 tsp.	2 tsp.
Salt	1 tsp.	1 tbsp.
Peppercorns, crushed	10	2 tbsp.

METHOD

1. Marinate shanks in vermouth, oil, lemon juice, shallots, garlic, herbs, salt, and pepper. Let stand at room temperature for at least 4 hours. Turn shanks once or twice and spoon marinade over them.
2. Broil shanks for about 30 minutes, turning frequently and basting with the marinade.

★ See picture, facing page.

BARBECUED LAMB SHANKS WITH VERMOUTH

The American
Lamb Council

VENISON MINCEMEAT
(A delightful filling for pies, tarts, and crepes)

YIELD:	1 GALLON	11 to 12 GALLONS
INGREDIENTS		
Lean Venison, cold, boiled, ground	2/3 cup	4 lb.
Red Apples, chopped, peeled	1-2/3 cups	10 lb.
Beef Suet, finely ground	1/4 cup	1-1/2 lb.
Currants	1/3 cup	2 lb.
Raisins	2/3 cup	4 lb.
Citron, finely sliced	1 tbsp.	1/2 lb.
Brown Sugar	1/3 cup	2 lb.
Granulated Sugar	1/3 cup	2 lb.
Venison Stock	1/3 cup	1 qt.
Molasses	1/4 cup	3 pt.
Ground Cloves	1/4 tsp.	1 tbsp.
Mace	1/4 tsp.	1 tbsp.
White Pepper	1/4 tsp.	1 tbsp.
Cinnamon	1 tsp.	10 tsp.
Lemons (juice and grated rind)	1/4 cup	3
Bourbon	2 tbsp.	1 pt.

METHOD
1. Combine all ingredients except lemon and bourbon; simmer slowly until flavors are well combined but apples are still crisp (about 30 minutes).
2. Add lemon and bourbon and allow the mixture to cool.

Denver Petroleum Club

Denver, Colorado

All of the members of the Denver Petroleum Club are connected with the petroleum industry in one way or another. Hence, many of the members have lived in Texas or Louisiana at some time, and most have traveled extensively abroad. The cuisine of the club reflects its members' backgrounds . . . it runs from Country Gravy (made by adding chopped onion and bacon to chicken fat and then adding as much flour as there is fat . . . right in the pans the chicken was fried in) to fine French fare.

Colorado is famous for its trout, and, although the club is able to get some fresh fish in Colorado, better luck and consistency come with the purchase of fast-frozen products. Even local Colorado trout must be purchased through a processor. The club credits a neighbor, the Garden of the Gods Club in Colorado Springs, with an interesting chef's secret. It is possible to make a Truite au Bleu with frozen trout! The secret is to let the frozen trout thaw, handling the fish as little as possible. When the trout have thawed, they are sprayed with vinegar and then poached. The blue color materializes and the body curves. It appears to be their natural body slime which causes the blue color, and wherever the trout are touched the slime is removed. You must be careful; fingerprints can betray you in the end.

CRAB ROLLS

(Dill and vermouth flavor crab folded inside a tender crepe)

YIELD:	5 PORTIONS	20 PORTIONS
INGREDIENTS		
Butter	1 tbsp.	2 oz. (1/4 cup)
Olive Oil	1-1/2 tsp.	2 tbsp.
Shallots, chopped	1 tbsp.	1/4 cup
King Crab Meat, canned, drained, diced, cartilage discarded	1 cup	4 cups
Parsley, chopped	2 tsp.	2 tbsp.
Dillweed	1/2 tsp.	2 tsp.
Salt	3/4 tsp.	1 tbsp.
White Pepper	1/4 tsp.	1 tsp.
Cayenne Pepper	dash	1/8 tsp.
Egg, Small, beaten	1	2
Dry White Vermouth	2 tbsp.	1/2 cup
Lemon Juice	2 tsp.	2 tbsp.
Crepes (recipe, p. 8)	10	40

METHOD

1. In saucepan, melt butter; add oil. Saute shallots until soft. Blend in crab, parsley, dillweed, salt, pepper, cayenne pepper, egg, vermouth, and lemon juice; simmer 5 minutes.
2. The purpose is to thicken the mixture and get rid of excess moisture, so that it does not run from the crepe. Taste and, if necessary, correct seasoning. Crab flavor should predominate.
3. Spoon a heaping tablespoon of crab mixture onto lower third portion of each flat crepe; spread it across, turn in the ends to keep mixture from falling out, and roll tightly.

Denver Petroleum Club

POLYNESIAN FRUIT SALAD

YIELD: 1 PORTION

INGREDIENTS		METHOD
Pineapple, hollowed-out	1 quarter (sliced crosswise)	1. In quarter of pineapple, alternate orange and pineapple slices.
Pineapple	1/2 slice	2. Alternate papaya and grapefruit sections around pineapple.
Orange	1/2 slice	
Papaya	1/2 slice	3. Top with 1 scoop of sherbet.
Grapefruit	1/2 slice	4. Garnish with melon balls, cherries, and mint leaves.
Sherbet	1 scoop	
Watermelon Balls	2	5. Serve with 1/2 toasted English muffin.
Honeydew Balls	2	
Red Cherry	2 halves	
Mint Leaves	1 sprig	

PEAR WALDORF SALAD

(Pears and apples are both featured in this beautiful salad entree)

YIELD:

INGREDIENTS	8 PORTIONS	24 PORTIONS	METHOD
Fresh Pear, peeled, diced	1 pt.	3 pt.	1. Combine pears, apples, celery, lemon juice, sugar, and mayonnaise.
Apples, diced	1 pt.	3 pt.	
Celery, thinly sliced	1 pt.	3 pt.	2. Line plate with lettuce leaves and place a cup of fruit mixture off-center.
Lemon Juice	1/4 cup	3/4 cup	
Sugar	2 tsp.	2 tbsp.	3. Garnish each salad with 3 apple wedges, 5 orange slices, 1 grape cluster, 2 dates or prunes, and 1 tbsp. chopped walnuts.
Mayonnaise	1 cup	3 cups	
Lettuce Leaves	as needed	as needed	
GARNISH			
Apple Wedges	24	72	
Orange Slices	40	120	
Grapes	8 clusters	24 clusters	
Dates *or* Prunes	16	48	
Walnuts, chopped	1/2 cup	1-1/2 cups	

WALDORF SALAD WITH JULIENNE HAM ★
(An entree salad that is popular year round)

YIELD:	4 PORTIONS	16 PORTIONS
INGREDIENTS		
Apples, diced	3 cups	3 qt.
Celery, sliced crosswise	1-1/2 cups	3 pt.
Cream Dressing (recipe, p. 236)	3/4 cup	1-1/2 pt.
Lettuce, Bite-sized	1-1/3 cups	5-1/3 cups
GARNISH		
Walnuts, chopped	4 tsp.	1/3 cup
Ham, trimmed, cut julienne	4 oz.	16 oz.
Watercress	4 sprigs	16 sprigs

METHOD
1. Do not peel apples if skin is tender; cut in dice and put in salt water until needed.
2. Slice celery thin and combine with well-drained apples.
3. Mix celery and apples with Cream Dressing just before serving.
4. Put about 1/3 cup bite-sized pieces of lettuce heart in double lettuce cup. Add 1 cup salad. Garnish with spoonful of dressing and chopped walnuts.
5. Place strips of julienne ham together on each side of salad. Garnish with watercress.
6. Serve with date muffins.

DENVER PETROLEUM CLUB DRESSING
(A mayonnaise base sharpened with lemon, Parmesan cheese, and garlic)

YIELD:	1 PINT	5 GALLONS
INGREDIENTS		
Mayonnaise	1-1/2 cups	4 gal.
Parmesan Cheese, grated	3 tbsp.	3-1/2 lb.
Lemon Juice	2 tsp.	2 cups
Pepper, freshly ground	1/4 tsp.	5 oz.
Garlic Powder	1/4 tsp.	5 oz.
Water	3 tbsp.	2 qt.
Salt	to taste	to taste
Flavor Enhancer	few grains	2 tbsp.

METHOD
1. Blend well until all ingredients are thoroughly mixed. The mixture should be the consistency of thick cream. Allow to marinate a few hours.

★ See picture, facing page.

WALDORF SALAD WITH JULIENNE HAM

The
Apple
Institute

LAMB CURRY BOMBAY STYLE ★

(Apples and white wine combine with Madras curry in this flavorful dish)

YIELD:	4 PORTIONS	24 PORTIONS
INGREDIENTS		
Flour	1/2 tsp.	1 tbsp.
Madras Curry	1/2 tsp.	1 tbsp.
Turmeric	1/2 tsp.	1 tbsp.
Lamb Shoulder, cubed	8 oz.	3 lb.
Onion, finely chopped	1/4	1-1/2
White Wine	2 tbsp.	6 oz.
Lamb Broth	1 cup	6 cups
Salt	to taste	to taste
Pepper	to taste	to taste
Apple	2	8 to 12
Chutney	1/2 tsp.	3 tsp.
Almonds, toasted	to garnish	to garnish
Rice	as needed	as needed
Peas	as needed	as needed

METHOD

1. Mix flour, curry, and turmeric with raw meat; saute quickly in very hot pan. Add onion and white wine; reduce. Add lamb broth. Cover the pan and allow mixture to simmer in oven at 350°F. for 1-1/4 hours, or until tender. Remove from stove and season to taste.
2. Slice 2 apple rings from each apple. Cut the balance of the apple into small diced pieces and mix with Lamb Curry. Serve apple ring filled with chutney. Sprinkle almonds on top of curry. Serve with rice and peas.

★ See picture, facing page.

LAMB CURRY BOMBAY STYLE

The
Apple
Institute

TURKEY TETRAZZINI

(Inexpensive, but glamorous, turkey and mushrooms nestle in spaghetti, with a sherry sauce over all and Parmesan cheese adding a bit of bite)

YIELD: **5 PORTIONS**   **20 PORTIONS**

INGREDIENTS			METHOD
Spaghetti, uncooked	1/4 lb.	1 lb.	
Butter	1-1/2 tbsp.	3 oz.	
Shortening	1 tbsp.	3 oz.	
Flour	2-1/2 tbsp.	6 oz.	
Chicken Stock	1 qt.	1 gal.	
Onion, finely chopped	1 tbsp.	2 oz.	
Butter	1 tbsp.	2 oz.	
Fresh Mushrooms, sliced	1/4 cup	6 oz.	
Half-and-Half	1/2 cup	1 pt.	
Dry Sherry	2 tbsp.	4 oz.	
Lemon Juice	1/2 tsp.	2 tsp.	
Celery Salt	dash	dash	
Cayenne Pepper	dash	dash	
Salt	to taste	to taste	
Pepper	to taste	to taste	
Turkey Meat, Light and Dark, cooked, diced	1-1/4 cups	2-1/2 lb.	
Parmesan Cheese, grated	3 tbsp.	6 oz.	
Dry Bread Crumbs	2 tbsp.	4 oz.	

METHOD

1. Cook spaghetti in salted water until just tender. Drain and rinse in cold water.
2. Make a roux by combining butter, shortening, and flour. Gradually add stock. Bring to a boil and cook gently for 1/2 hour.
3. Saute onion in butter. Add mushrooms; saute until tender.
4. Add onion, mushrooms, half-and-half, and sherry to sauce. Season with lemon juice, celery salt, cayenne, salt, and pepper.
5. Put heaping 1/2 cup of spaghetti in oval shirred egg dish. Add a layer of diced turkey. Add sauce.
6. Mix cheese with crumbs and sprinkle a heaping tablespoon over entire surface.
7. Dot with butter and bake in oven at 450°F., until brown and bubbling.
8. Serve with tossed green salad or sliced tomatoes sprinkled with basil and minced fresh parsley.

CHICKEN VELOUTE WITH MUSHROOMS

(Serve with rice, noodles, waffles, or toast, or in puff-paste shells)

YIELD:	6 PORTIONS	24 PORTIONS
INGREDIENTS		
Chicken Breasts,		
Whole	3	12
Water	1-1/2 qt.	1-1/2 gal.
Dry White Wine	1 cup	1 qt.
Carrots	2	8
Onions	2	8
Parsley	4 sprigs	16 sprigs
Celery	2 ribs	8 ribs
Salt	2 tsp.	2 tbsp.
CHICKEN VELOUTE		
Butter	6 tbsp.	3/4 lb.
Fresh Mushrooms,		
Small, sliced	12	48
Flour	5 tbsp.	1-1/4 cups
Chicken Stock	2 cups	2 qt.
Heavy Cream	1 cup	1 qt.
Brandy	2 tbsp.	1/2 cup
Parsley, chopped	2 tbsp.	1/2 cup
Salt	1-1/2 tsp.	2 tbsp.

METHOD

1. To prepare chicken, place chicken breasts and next 7 ingredients in a pot; cover and simmer over medium heat for 35 minutes, or until chicken is tender. Cool. Remove skin and bones. Dice chicken. Save chicken stock for veloute sauce.

CHICKEN VELOUTE

2. To make Chicken Veloute, melt 1/3 of the butter in saucepan. Saute mushrooms for 5 minutes. Remove from heat.

3. In another deep saucepan, melt remaining butter over medium heat; sift in flour, blending into a smooth, golden paste.

4. Remove from heat and add heated chicken stock, a little at a time, beating with a wire whisk into a smooth sauce. Return to heat; simmer 10 minutes, slowly blending in the cream, then the brandy, parsley, and salt.

5. Cook until thickened. Stir in mushrooms. Blend well. Save one-third of the sauce to pass in a sauceboat at the table. Blend the diced chicken into the remaining sauce. Taste for seasoning

CREAMED BROCCOLI TRIANGLES

(Sherried broccoli folded into crepes heavily sprinkled with Parmesan, then finished in the oven)

YIELD: 10 PORTIONS   20 PORTIONS

INGREDIENTS		
Water	3/4 cup	1-1/2 cups
Salt	1/2 tsp.	1 tsp.
Broccoli, Frozen, Chopped	1 pkg. (12 oz.)	2 pkg. (12 oz.)
Butter	2-1/2 tbsp.	5 tbsp.
Flour	2 tbsp.	4 tbsp.
Light Cream, warm	3/4 cup	1-1/2 cups
Sherry	1 tbsp.	2 tbsp.
Salt	3/4 tsp.	1-1/2 tsp.
Black Pepper	1/4 tsp.	1/2 tsp.
Parmesan Cheese, grated	1/2 cup	1 cup
Crepes (recipe, p. 102)	10	20

METHOD

1. Bring water to boil in a saucepan. Add salt and frozen broccoli. Cover and simmer for 10 minutes, or until tender, being careful not to overcook. Drain well.
2. Melt butter in a saucepan over medium heat; stir in flour and cook 2 minutes, stirring constantly, until you have a smooth paste.
3. Remove from heat and slowly stir in the warm cream, sherry, salt, and pepper and half the cheese. Simmer over medium heat, stirring, until you have obtained a smooth, thick sauce. Taste for seasoning. Blend in the drained broccoli.
4. Spoon a heaping tbsp. of broccoli mixture onto the center of a crepe. Fold crepe in half, then fold again to form a triangle.
5. Butter an ovenproof dish; arrange broccoli crepes side by side without touching. Sprinkle with remaining cheese; dot with butter. Place in preheated oven at 375°F. for 15 minutes.

ROYAL SWEET POTATOES

(Orange and sherry add their flavor to sweet potatoes or yams)

YIELD:	5 PORTIONS	50 PORTIONS
INGREDIENTS		
Sweet Potatoes	5	50
Brown Sugar	1/3 cup	3 cups
Granulated Sugar	1/3 cup	3 cups
Salt	to taste	to taste
Cornstarch	2 tsp.	1/2 cup
Orange Juice, Frozen, re-constituted	3/4 cup	2 qt.
Orange Rind, grated	1 tsp.	1/4 cup
Sherry	1/4 cup	2 cups

METHOD

1. Boil sweet potatoes in jackets until tender, 30 to 35 minutes. Peel and cut in half or into thick slices.
2. Combine sugars, salt, and cornstarch. Stir in orange juice and rind. Simmer until thick and smooth, about five minutes. Remove from heat.
3. Add sherry and pour over potatoes.
4. Bake, covered, in oven at 350°F. for 20 minutes. Remove cover; bake 15 minutes more.
5. Allow 2 halves, or slices to equal 2 halves, per serving.

BLEU CHEESE AND CHOPPED BACON SANDWICH

(Two triangles of this sandwich make a nice garnish for a vegetable luncheon salad)

YIELD:	5 SANDWICHES	25 SANDWICHES
INGREDIENTS		
Bleu Cheese	1/4 cup	10 oz.
Philadelphia-style Cream Cheese	1/4 cup	10 oz.
Half-and-Half	2 tbsp.	5 oz.
Bottled Steak Sauce	1/2 tsp.	2 tsp.
Liquid Hot Pepper Seasoning	a drop	few drops
Bacon, crisp-fried, crumbled	4 tbsp.	3/4 lb.
Bread (Cracked or Sprouted Wheat preferred)	10 slices	50 slices

METHOD

1. Blend cheeses with half-and-half until smooth; add seasonings. Add the crumbled bacon, blending well.
2. Spread No. 24 scoop on slice of bread. Top with slice of buttered bread.
3. Cut in triangles or fingers and serve with cup of soup on "Soup 'n 'Sandwich" luncheon.

BAKED CHEESE SOUFFLE SANDWICH

(A meatless luncheon dish that can be assembled long before baking)

YIELD:	5 PORTIONS	25 PORTIONS
INGREDIENTS		
White Bread, day old, trimmed	10 slices	50 slices
American Cheese	5 slices	25 slices
Eggs, Large	4	20
Milk	3 cups	3 qt. plus 3 cups
Worcestershire Sauce	2/3 tsp.	1 tbsp.
Liquid Hot Pepper Seasoning	3 drops	1 tsp.
Salt	1-1/4 tsp.	2 tbsp.
White Pepper	1/2 tsp.	2-1/2 tsp.

METHOD

1. Lay half of the slices of bread in greased long steam table pan (No. 100 pan). Top each slice with slice of cheese. Top with remaining slices of bread.
2. Beat eggs slightly, as for a custard. Add milk and seasonings. Pour over the sandwiches.
3. Bake in oven at 350°F. for about 1-1/2 to 1-3/4 hours, or until custard is set and top is golden brown. If top is not golden brown, run under broiler quickly.
4. Let sandwiches set about 15 minutes before serving.
5. Serve with slices of apple, pear, or tomato and watercress.

Note   These sandwiches hold well on the steam table.

APRICOT FRITTERS ★

(A nice garniture for ham or sausages, or a light luncheon entree served with orange sauce and crisp, fried bacon)

YIELD:	10 FRITTERS	60 FRITTERS
INGREDIENTS		
Egg, separated	1	6
Milk	1-1/3 cup	2 qt.
Cake Flour	2/3 cup	2 lb.
Baking Powder	1 tbsp.	3 oz.
Granulated Sugar	2 tbsp plus 2 tsp.	1/2 pt.
Salt	pinch	1 tsp.
Vanilla	few drops	1 tsp.
Apricot Halves, well-drained	10	60

METHOD

1. Separate eggs; beat yolks slightly.
2. Add milk to yolks; mix.
3. Add flour, baking powder, sugar, and salt; beat until batter is perfectly smooth.
4. Fold in beaten egg whites and vanilla.
5. Dip fruit into flour to coat lightly, then dip into fritter batter. Drain slightly and fry in peanut oil to cover at 350° to 360°F.
6. Turn the fritters once and fry to an even brown on both sides. (These will hold on the steam table for about 30 minutes.)

★ See picture, facing page.

APRICOT FRITTERS

California
Apricot
Advisory Board

Fort Worth Club

Fort Worth, Texas

Will Rogers loved the chili they make at the Fort Worth Club, but one day when he was enjoying chili and corn bread in his room at the club he decided there was just one thing wrong. The spoon was not big enough. He told the waiter to go to the kitchen and bring him a spoon. A really big spoon. A scoop. Well, the waiter did and, according to reports, old Will just stuffed that chili into his mouth and grinned.

Members of the club agree with Will's taste in food. They like basic dishes . . . not continental and not exotic. At parties they favor Beef Wellington and escargots, but for day-to-day eating, members prefer a menu featuring down-to-earth American fare sprinkled with some dishes from Mexico, some from northern Italy, some German food, and some Basque . . . all of it adapted to "Texanize."

PICADILLO DIP

(Potato chips, corn chips, or raw vegetables can accompany this unusual dip)

YIELD:	3 CUPS	1-1/2 GALLONS
INGREDIENTS		
Shallots	3	24
or		
Scallions	6	48
Butter	1/4 cup	2 cups
Curry Powder	1 tbsp.	1/2 cup
Sour Cream	1-1/2 cups	3 qt.
Pickle Relish	1 cup	8 cups
Chutney	2 tbsp.	1 cup
Worcestershire Sauce	1 tbsp.	1/2 cup
Salt	1/2 tsp.	4 tsp.
Cayenne Pepper	1/8 tsp.	1 tsp.

METHOD

1. Saute shallots or scallions in butter until soft but not browned.
2. Add curry powder and blend well over low heat.
3. Blend in remaining ingredients. Refrigerate.

FORT WORTH CLUB SEASONING

(A basting liquid to flavor poultry and game birds while roasting)

YIELD:	1 QUART, 1 CUP
INGREDIENTS	
Salad Oil	1 qt.
Paprika	1/2 cup
Flavor Enhancer	5 tbsp.
Salt	3 tbsp.
Onion Salt	2 tbsp.
Black Pepper	1 tbsp.

METHOD

Combine all ingredients in a covered container; shake well.

WILL ROGERS CHILI

(A real Southwest chili, with lots of authority)

YIELD:	5 PORTIONS	20 PORTIONS
INGREDIENTS		
Beef Chuck, coarsely chopped	1-1/4 lb.	5 lb.
Chili Peppers, Dried, finely ground	3	12
Onion, Large, minced	1/2	2
Garlic, minced	1/2 small clove	1 clove
Granulated Sugar	1 tbsp.	2 oz. (4 to 5 tbsp.)
Paprika	1 tbsp.	4 tbsp.
Salt	1/2 tbsp.	2 tbsp.
Ground Cumino	1/4 tsp.	1 tsp.
Cayenne Pepper	1/8 tsp.	1/2 tsp.
Flour	2 tbsp.	1/2 cup
Beef Stock	1 pint	1/2 gal.

METHOD

1. Braise beef until half done. Add chili peppers, onion, and garlic; saute. Add seasonings and flour; cook 5 minutes. Stir in beef stock and simmer slowly for 15 to 20 minutes, making sure that all flour lumps have been dissolved.

WHITE WING DOVES

(Dainty birds served in a Burgundy sauce on rice pilaf make an elegant entree)

YIELD:	6 PORTIONS	24 PORTIONS
INGREDIENTS		
Doves, plucked or skinned, drawn	12	48
Flour	1/2 cup	2 cups
Salt	1/2 tsp.	2 tsp.
Pepper, freshly ground	1/4 tsp.	1 tsp.
Thyme	1/2 tsp.	2 tsp.
Marjoram	1/2 tsp.	2 tsp.
Butter	1/2 cup	2 cups
Shallots, minced	1 tbsp.	1/4 cup
Half-and-Half	3 cups	3 qt.
Chicken Base	1 tsp.	1 tbsp. plus 1 tsp.
Burgundy	1 cup	1 qt.

METHOD

1. Dust doves with combined flour, salt, pepper, thyme, and marjoram. Lightly brown doves in butter and remove from pan.
2. Saute shallots in pan butter, then use seasoned flour left from dusting birds to completely absorb drippings. Add remaining ingredients. Stir constantly with a wire whip allowing the mixture to simmer for 10 minutes. If sauce is too heavy, add more cream. Correct seasonings.
3. Strain sauce. Add the browned birds, cover, and simmer for 40 minutes. Remove birds and again strain the sauce.
4. Serve birds on rice pilaf garnished with the shell of half a lime filled with currant jelly. Present sauce on the side.

CORNISH HENS ALEXANDRA

(Rubbed with a special seasoning and basted with a special sauce, these little hens are indeed "special")

YIELD: 1 QUART SAUCE

INGREDIENTS

		METHOD
Rock Cornish Game Hens		1. Rub game hens with *Fort Worth Club Seasoning.*
Fort Worth Club Seasoning	to taste	
Butter, melted	as needed	2. Cook hens for 45 minutes in oven at 350°F., basting every 10 minutes with sauce made by combining *Sauce* ingredients.
SAUCE		
Catsup	1 pt.	3. In the last 5 minutes, brush with butter.
Orange Marmalade	1 pt.	4. Serve on bed of wild rice and garnish with spiced pickled peaches.
Worcestershire Sauce	1 tbsp.	
Soy Sauce	1 tbsp.	
Cayenne Pepper	1/8 tsp.	

DOVER SOLE WITH SHRIMP

(Sole glazed with Hollandaise is topped with shrimp sauteed in butter and lemon)

YIELD: 1 PORTION

INGREDIENTS

		METHOD
Fillet of Dover Sole	1	1. Season sole with salt and pepper; dust with flour.
Salt	to taste	
Pepper	to taste	2. Brown gently in butter; sprinkle with lemon juice.
Flour	1 tbsp.	
Butter	1 tbsp.	3. Brown shrimp in butter; add lemon juice.
Lemon Juice	1 tsp.	4. Glaze sole with Hollandaise under salamander or broiler.
Shrimp	3	
Hollandaise Sauce (recipe, p. 226)	as needed	5. Garnish top of each glazed sole with 3 shrimp.
		6. Serve with a lemon basket of caviar, tomato topped with white asparagus tips, and broccoli florettes amandine.

MEXICAN CORN MUFFINS

(Kernels of corn combine with hot peppers, onion, and pimiento to make these corn meal muffins a delightful, hot bread)

YIELD:	1 DOZEN	4 DOZEN
INGREDIENTS		
Yellow Corn Meal	1 cup	4 cups
All-Purpose Flour, sifted	1/2 cup	2 cups
Baking Powder	1-1/2 tsp.	2 tbsp.
Granulated Sugar	1 tsp.	4 tsp.
Salt	1/8 tsp.	1/2 tsp.
Eggs, beaten	2	8
Buttermilk	1 cup	1 qt.
Corn, Cream-Style	1 cup	1 qt.
Salad Oil	1/2 cup	2 cups
Jalapeno Peppers, Medium-Sized, finely chopped	2	8
Onion, Medium-Sized, finely chopped	1	4
Pimiento, finely chopped	2 tbsp.	1/2 cup

METHOD

1. Stir together corn meal, flour, baking powder, sugar, and salt.
2. Gently stir into combined eggs and buttermilk.
3. Add remaining ingredients, mixing only until combined.
4. Spoon into well-greased muffin pans and bake 20 minutes in preheated oven at 450°F.

Friars Club

New York, New York

The first floor of the Friars Club's New York brownstone, referred to as "The Monastery," houses what must be the tiniest bar in New York. There is also a dining room seating 120 for normal meal service, but 200 elbow-to-fork once a month when the Club holds a "Salute" to some entertainer, usually a member. These packed events turn into love-ins, with everyone getting up and performing as a part of the impromptu show. A distinct contrast to the famous Friars' "roasts."

The Friars are gentle to the lady performers. . .those they honor are never roasted, they are given a "testimonial dinner." To date there have been two ladies so honored—both comediennes—Lucille Ball and Carol Burnett. The roasts are strictly stag and confined to members only. The profits from both the testimonial dinners and the roasts go to works of charity.

Of the club's 1,100 members, two-thirds are connected with "show-biz" in some form and one-third come from "outside." That balance has been maintained since the club's inception in 1904. Since show people are night people, the club is open around the clock and serves as a meeting ground for the entertainment industry.

BLACK BEAN SOUP A LA SAN JUAN

(A hearty specialty of Puerto Rico)

YIELD:	3 QUARTS	3 GALLONS
INGREDIENTS		
Black Beans*	1/2 lb.	2 lb.
Beef Stock	3 qt.	3 gal.
Shortening	3 tbsp.	6 oz.
Onion, Medium-Sized, chopped	3/4	3
White Celery, sliced	3/4 rib	3 ribs
Garlic, minced	1/2 clove	2 cloves
Pimiento	1/2	2
Prepared Mustard	1/2 tbsp.	2 tbsp.
Salt	to taste	to taste
Pepper	to taste	to taste
Rice, cooked	1/4 cup	1 cup
Onion, minced	2 tbsp.	1/2 cup

*If beans are dried, soak them in water for a few hours.

METHOD

1. Cook beans in beef stock until tender.
2. When cooking is completed, add more stock to make 3 qt. or 3 gal. Set aside.
3. In another pan, heat shortening; add onion, celery, and garlic; brown lightly and add to beans.
4. Stir in pimiento, mustard, and salt and pepper to taste.
5. Simmer 15 minutes on low heat.
6. Serve hot and garnish each cup with 1 tsp. rice and 1/2 tsp. minced onion.

FRIARS CLUB CLAM CHOWDER

(A hard act to follow with tomatoes as a supporting actor)

YIELD:	3 QUARTS	6 GALLONS
INGREDIENTS		
Hard-Shell Clams	1-1/2 doz.	12 doz.
Salt Pork, diced	3 oz.	1-1/2 lb.
Onion, Small, chopped	1	6
Leek, thinly sliced	1	8
Garlic Clove, minced	1 small clove	6 cloves
Green Pepper, Small, chopped	1	6
Carrot, Small diced	1	6
Potatoes, diced	1 qt.	2 gal.
Celery, diced	1 cup	2 qt.
Salt	1/2 tbsp.	2 oz.
Clam Broth	2-1/2 cups	1-1/4 gal.
Tomatoes	1/2 cup	1 No. 10 can
Catsup	3 tbsp.	2 14-oz. bottles
Black Pepper, freshly ground	to taste	1/2 oz.
Thyme	1/2 tsp.	2 tbsp.
Bay Leaf	1/3	3
Whole Cloves	2	16

METHOD

1. Cook clams, saving the liquor. Mince hard parts of clams and chop the soft parts coarsely.
2. Saute salt pork until golden brown. Stir in onion, leek, garlic, and green pepper; saute 5 minutes.
3. Add minced clams, carrot, potatoes, celery, salt, and clam broth. Bring to a boil; reduce heat, cover, and simmer 10 minutes.
4. Add chopped clams and enough clam liquor to make 3 qt. or 6 gal. Stir in tomatoes, catsup, black pepper, and a *bouquet garni* made of thyme, bay leaf, and cloves tied in cheesecloth.
5. Simmer for 1 hour.

BROCHETTE OF FILLET OF BEEF

(Beef marinated in Burgundy alternates with mushrooms and green peppers on a skewer. Yellow rice, June peas, and Bordelaise Sauce complete the dish)

YIELD:	6 PORTIONS	24 PORTIONS
INGREDIENTS		
Fillet of Beef	1	4
Salt	1-1/2 tsp.	2 tbsp.
Black Pepper	1/2 tsp.	2 tsp.
Thyme	1/4 tsp.	1 tsp.
Burgundy	1/2 cup	2 cups
Green Peppers, Medium-Sized	3	12
Mushrooms, Fresh *or* Canned	18	72
Butter, melted	1/2 cup	2 cups
Yellow Rice, cooked	3 cups	6 lb.
June Peas, Small	1 17-oz. can	4 lb.
Bordelaise Sauce (recipe, p. 224)	1-1/2 cups	6 cups

METHOD

1. Cut the beef into 1-1/2-inch cubes. Place in a large bowl and season with salt, pepper, and thyme. Stir in wine and set aside for an hour.
2. Cut green peppers into 1-1/2-inch squares. Blanch in boiling water until tender but firm. Drain and cool.
3. Clean mushrooms.
4. Fill the skewers allowing 5 beef cubes, 3 green pepper squares, and 3 mushrooms per serving. Brush with butter and cook evenly.
5. On a 10-inch oval dish arrange 4 oz. of rice. Lay the brochette on the rice, pull out the skewer, and garnish plate with hot June peas.
6. Serve Bordelaise Sauce on the side.

ARROZ CON POLLO

(The Spanish way with chicken, peas, and rice)

YIELD:	5 PORTIONS	20 PORTIONS
INGREDIENTS		
Olive *or* Corn Oil	1/2 cup	2 cups
Onion, Large, chopped	1/2	2
Green Chili Pepper, chopped	1/2	2
Garlic, chopped	1 clove	5 cloves
Tomato Paste	1-1/4 oz.	5 oz.
Saffron	1/4 tsp.	1 tsp.
Bay Leaf, Small	1/4	1
White Pepper	1/4 tsp.	1 tsp.
Fryers, cut in 6 pieces (do not use backs)	2-1/2 (2-1/2 lb.)	10 (2-1/2 lb.)
Chicken Consomme	1-1/4 qt.	5 qt.
Rice, Long Grain	1-1/4 lb.	5 lb.
Salt	to taste	to taste
Green Peas, cooked	1-3/4 cups	7 cups
Pimiento	1 tbsp.	1/4 cup

METHOD

1. Pour oil into a heavy pot; heat; add chopped onion, pepper, and garlic; saute for 5 minutes.
2. Stir in tomato paste, saffron, bay leaf, and pepper.
3. Add chicken parts and cook 10 minutes.
4. Stir in consomme and rice. Taste and add salt as needed during cooking. Cover pot and bring to a boil. Reduce heat to low and cook until all liquid is absorbed. Uncover during final 10 minutes of cooking.
5. Garnish with green peas and pimiento.

FILLET OF SOLE VERONIQUE

(Sole poached in wine and served with white grapes)

YIELD:	1 PORTION	6 PORTIONS	24 PORTIONS

INGREDIENTS				METHOD
Fillet of Sole, Large	1	6	24	
Salt	to taste	to taste	to taste	
Fish Stock	1/4 cup	1 cup	1 qt.	
Dry White Wine	2 tbsp.	1/2 cup	2 cups	
White Grapes, skinned, seeded	1/4 cup	1 cup	4 cups	
Butter	1 tbsp.	1/4 cup	1 cup	

METHOD

1. Flatten fillets lightly with the flat of a knife and fold them in half; season with salt. Lay the folded fillets side by side in a buttered pan.
2. Pour fish stock and wine over the fish. Cook gently for 10 minutes.
3. Move fillets to a platter and garnish with grapes.
4. Reduce the cooking liquor over high heat to 1/4 of its original volume. Remove from fire and swirl in the butter; adjust seasoning.
5. Pour sauce over fillets and grapes; set the platter under the broiler to glaze the sauce.

Friars Club

Glen Oaks Country Club

Old Westbury, New York

The club's original clubhouse was the home of William K. Vanderbilt on his country estate. Now, 50 years later, the club has moved into a new clubhouse just across the line in Nassau County.

Seafood is a favorite at Glen Oaks, and the chef has found a way to substitute matzoh meal for sand in steamed clams! The matzoh serves to clean the sand out of the clams and make them more pleasant to eat. The steamers are scrubbed and then left in clean water sprinkled with matzoh meal—2 cups of matzoh to 1 bushel of steamers. The live clams continue feeding, eat the meal, and eliminate the sand. Later, the matzoh cooks as the clams steam. The meal makes the clams sweeter, fuller, and, best of all, free of sand.

Broiled lobster is another favorite at Glen Oaks. Two-pound lobsters are split, drawn, and brushed with butter. They are then heavily sprinkled with a mixture of ground bread crumbs, butter, parsley, salt, pepper, and lots of paprika. The small legs from the side of the lobster are removed and broiled on top of the crumb mixture, as they are succulent and moist and help keep the lobster from becoming too dry. More clarified butter goes on top.

STUFFED CLAMS

(An Italian recipe for lovers of oregano and garlic)

INGREDIENTS		METHOD
Basic Recipe (recipe, p. 76)	1 recipe	1. While preparing Basic Recipe, stir in oregano, garlic, and thyme before the bread crumbs are added.
Oregano	3 tbsp.	
Garlic, finely chopped	3 tbsp.	
Thyme	1 tsp.	2. Cover clams in their shells with the mixture and bake in oven at 400°F. for 15 minutes. Serve with lemon wedges.
Clams	as desired	

SAUERKRAUT STRUDEL

(Flaky layers of strudel hold a delicious sauerkraut mixture in this Bavarian specialty)

YIELD:	6 PORTIONS	25 PORTIONS	
INGREDIENTS			METHOD
Sauerkraut	1-1/4 lb.	5 lb.	1. Wash sauerkraut and drain well. Melt butter in heavy skillet and saute diced onion until golden brown.
Butter	1/4 lb.	1 lb.	
Onion, Large, diced	1/2	2	
Raisins	1/2 cup	1 lb.	2. Add sauerkraut, raisins, brown sugar, and caraway seeds; cover and cook 30 minutes. Cool.
Brown Sugar	1/2 cup	1 lb.	
Caraway Seeds	2 tsp.	3 tbsp.	
Filo Pastry (Strudel Leaves)	as needed	as needed	3. Lay out 2 filo pastry sheets, one on top of the other; sprinkle with a few bread crumbs. Arrange cooked sauerkraut at one end of the dough and roll up. Repeat until sauerkraut is all used. Lay rolls out on papered or lightly greased sheet pans. Brush with egg wash and sprinkle with sesame seeds.
Bread Crumbs	1/4 cup	1 cup	
Egg Wash*	1/2 egg	2 eggs	
Sesame Seeds	1 tsp.	1 tbsp.	4. Bake in oven at 350°F. until lightly browned. When cool, slice into portions.
			5. Allow 2 halves, or slices to equal 2 halves, per serving.

* Egg wash is prepared by adding 1 tbsp. cold water to 1 small egg, beaten.

Note This unusual kraut mixture will keep a long time in the refrigerator.

BURGUNDY CHEESE AND NUT MOLD

(An attractive addition to a cheese tray or serve with fruit for an elegant dessert)

YIELD:	2 POUNDS	12 POUNDS
INGREDIENTS		
Cheddar Cheese	1-2/3 lb.	10 lb.
Pistachio Nuts,		
salted, shelled	1 cup	2 lb.
Burgundy, Dry	1/3 cup	2 cups

METHOD
1. Remove cheese from package and pack some into bottom of mold.
2. Sprinkle with nuts and pour a little wine on top.
3. Repeat process until mold is filled; pour remaining wine on top.
4. Cover and refrigerate for 2 or more days; unmold.
5. Extra nuts can be used to trim the outside; however, too many will spoil the ripple effect of the red wine and cheese.

CHICKEN GIBLET PATE

(Serve as a dip at the bar, use for canapes, or serve as an appetizer on a lettuce leaf garnished with a cherry pepper and buttered black bread)

YIELD:	1 POUND	8 POUNDS
INGREDIENTS		
Chicken Giblets		
and Hearts,		
well-cooked	10 oz.	5 lb.
Cheddar Cheese,		
Sharp	2 oz.	1 lb.
Swiss Cheese (end		
scraps, etc.)	2 oz.	1 lb.
Onion, Large	1/4	2
Celery, finely		
chopped	1/2 rib	4 or 5 ribs
Anchovy Paste	1/2 oz.	4 to 6 oz.
Mayonnaise	1/4 cup	1 qt.
Black Pepper	as needed	as needed
Salt	to taste	to taste

METHOD
1. Put giblets, cheeses, onion, and celery through food grinder with fine holes.
2. Stir in anchovy paste and mayonnaise.
3. Season to taste.

PUREE OF JUNE PEA SOUP

(This unusual soup made of tender green peas flavored with bacon is garnished with julienne strips of lettuce)

YIELD:	2 QUARTS	2 GALLONS
INGREDIENTS		
June Peas	3 cups	1 No. 10 can
Bacon, finely diced	1/4 lb.	1 lb.
Onion, finely diced	1/2	2
All-Purpose Flour	1/2 cup	1/2 lb.
Chicken Stock	1 qt.	4 qt.
Salt	to taste	to taste
Black Pepper	to taste	to taste
Lettuce Leaves, Dark Green	2	3 or 4

METHOD
1. Drain peas and reserve liquid.
2. Put peas through food grinder, rotary sieve, or blender; set aside.
3. Fry bacon and onion together until bacon is crisp and onion is browned.
4. Add flour; stir until smooth. Add liquid from peas and the puree.
5. Continue to stir, adding chicken stock a little at a time until desired consistency is reached. Season. Serve garnished with julienne strips of lettuce.

MINIETTES

(Deep-fried stuffing balls can be served as hors d'oeuvre or as an accompaniment for fish)

YIELD:	16 BALLS	256 BALLS
INGREDIENTS		
Basic Recipe (recipe, p. 76)	2 cups	2 gal.
Flour	1/2 cup	2 qt.
Egg	1	16
Water, cold	1 tbsp.	1 cup
Bread Crumbs	1 cup	1 gal.
Fat for deep frying	as needed	as needed

METHOD
1. Scoop Basic Recipe into small balls, about 2 tbsp. or smaller in size.
2. Roll first in flour, then in combined egg and cold water, and finally in bread crumbs.
3. Deep fry and serve hot.

LOBSTER STUFFING ★

(An elegant stuffing for baked fish, fillets, or turkey)

YIELD:	2 CUPS	2 GALLONS
INGREDIENTS		
Basic Recipe		
(recipe below)	2 cups	2 gal.
Nutmeg	1/3 tsp.	1 tbsp.
Spanish Paprika	1/8 tsp.	4 to 6 tbsp.
South African		
Rock Lobster	as desired	as desired

METHOD

1. Stir nutmeg, paprika, and lobster into Basic Recipe before combining with bread crumbs.

CHEF PEARSALL'S BASIC RECIPE FOR SEAFOOD STUFFING

(Seafood stock flavors fried bread crumbs to make a light, fluffy stuffing)

YIELD:	2 CUPS	2 GALLONS
INGREDIENTS		
Onion, Large		
chopped	1 tbsp.	2
Clarified Butter	1 tbsp.	1 lb.
All-Purpose Flour	1 tbsp.	1 lb.
Lobster Stock	1-1/2 cups	6 qt.
Salt	to taste	to taste
White Pepper	to taste	to taste
Bread Crumbs,		
fried	as needed	as needed
Butter *or* Margarine,		
melted, *or* Oil	1/4 cup	1 qt.

METHOD

1. Saute onion in butter. Stir in flour. Stirring constantly, gradually add stock until mixture reaches the consistency of very light cream sauce.
2. Add salt and pepper to taste. Gradually stir in bread crumbs until the mixture is the consistency of stiff mashed potatoes.
3. Beat in liquid fat to make mixture light and fluffy.

★ See picture, facing page.

LOBSTER STUFFING

South
African
Rock
Lobster

GLEN OAKS CLUB SALAD

(Toss portions to order and enjoy for lunch)

YIELD:	1 PORTION	20 PORTIONS	
INGREDIENTS			METHOD
Turkey Breast, cooked, cut julienne	4 oz.	5 lb.	1. Toss first 3 ingredients together with dressing selected by guest.
Tomato, Small, chopped	1	20	2. Garnish with bacon slices.
Iceberg Lettuce, cut julienne	1/4 head	5 heads	
Mayonnaise, Russian, *or* French Dressing	as needed	as needed	
Bacon, crisp fried	3 slices	60 slices	

CHICKEN JUBILEE ★

(A low-calorie luncheon entree)

YIELD:	1 PORTION	24 PORTIONS	
INGREDIENTS			METHOD
Chicken Breast, poached, cut julienne	3 oz.	5 lb.	1. Toss first 6 ingredients together and garnish with parsley.
Iceberg Lettuce, crisp, cut julienne	1/4 head	6 heads	
Salad Oil, Light	2 tbsp.	3 cups	
Fresh Lemon Juice	1 tbsp.	1-1/2 cups	
Salt	to taste	to taste	
White Pepper	to taste	to taste	
Parsley	to garnish	to garnish	

★ See picture, facing page.

CHICKEN JUBILEE

Western
Iceberg
Lettuce, Inc.

Harmonie Club

New York, New York

Until 1893 only German was spoken at the Harmonie Club, and the records were kept in German script. The membership was, and remains, almost entirely of German ancestry. Founded in 1852, the club is the second oldest social club in the city. The Harmonie Club's 6 founders envisioned a fraternity bound together by mutual social interests, the chief of which was song recitals. Hence the club's original name, the *Gessellschaft Harmonie*.

Music is no longer the club's central theme, but the membership remains primarily concerned with the arts, among them a traditional interest in fine food.

The club's stated philosophy for designing a banquet or gourmet dinner is that it should follow, more or less, the classic tradition of having a good assortment of courses planned so that guests enjoy variety without becoming satiated. The portions should be small, and only one dish, at the most, should have a heavy sauce. Members also feel that the best wine should not be saved for the cheese but enjoyed earlier in the meal while the taste buds are livelier.

In selecting shrimp for a formal dinner to be given for an international gourmet group at the club, the original plan had been to serve Icelandic lobster tails. They were not available, and a choice arose between 2 kinds of shrimp, Gulf and Spanish. The shrimp were so different from each other in taste and appearance that the club has since offered them together whenever possible. They are split in the shell, broiled, and served side by side with Butter Sauce or as Crevettes au Beurre (see recipe, page 82), a clever idea for an unusual hot shrimp appetizer.

STRACIATELLA ALLA ROMANA

(An Italian cheese soup with cooked egg adding colorful shreds of texture)

YIELD:	1-1/2 QUARTS	1 GALLON
INGREDIENTS		
Eggs	3	9
Romano *or* Parmesan Cheese, finely grated	3 tbsp.	1/2 cup
Parsley, minced	2 tbsp.	1/3 cup
Chicken Broth	6 cups	1 gal.

METHOD
1. Beat eggs until frothy.
2. Stir cheese and parsley into eggs (flavor of soup will depend principally on whether cheese is freshly grated).
3. Bring broth to rolling boil and pour egg mixture into it, stirring steadily until eggs set.

LA CARRE D'AGNEAU SOUS BOIS

(Rack of lamb flavored with garlic and beautifully crusted with a fine coating of bread crumbs)

YIELD:	6 PORTIONS	24 PORTIONS
INGREDIENTS		
Rack of Lamb	1	4
Garlic, finely chopped	2 cloves	8 cloves
Bread Crumbs	3/4 cup	3 cups
Parsley, chopped	1/2 cup	2 cups
Butter	as needed	as needed
Salt	to taste	to taste
Pepper, freshly cracked	to taste	to taste

METHOD
1. Trim and wrap bone ends of chops with foil.
2. Blend garlic, bread crumbs, and parsley.
3. Rub roast well with butter, salt, and pepper.
4. Place on rack in roasting pan and roast in oven at 375°F., basting every 10 minutes. After 20 minutes test meat for internal temperature. Remove from oven.
5. Skim fat from pan juices. Mix pan juices with crumb mixture and spread even film of crumb mixture over lamb. Return to oven until nicely browned and done.

CREVETTES AU BEURRE

(Giant shrimp sauteed in the shell and served with a Soy-Butter Sauce)

YIELD:	6 PORTIONS	24 PORTIONS
INGREDIENTS		
Shrimp, Jumbo-Sized	12	48
Oil	3 tbsp.	3/4 cup
Salt	1/2 tsp.	2 tsp.
White Pepper	1/4 tsp.	1 tsp.
Butter	3/4 cup	3 cups (1-1/2 lb.)
Soy Sauce	1 tbsp.	1/4 cup

METHOD

1. Split shrimp, shells and all, lengthwise in half. Clean well and let shrimp remain in halved shells.
2. Heat oil in heavy skillet; arrange shrimp shell-side down in pan and cook gently for 5 minutes.
3. Season, cover, and let shrimp simmer until tender, 5 to 10 minutes.
4. Serve shells with clarified butter* flavored with soy sauce.

*To clarify butter: melt butter, remove from heat, and allow solids to drop to bottom of pan. Pour off clear butter and use remainder for cooking.

BLUEBERRY BUCKLE ★

(Old-fashioned blueberry pudding with a streusel topping)

YIELD:	8 PORTIONS	24 PORTIONS
INGREDIENTS		
Granulated Sugar	3/4 cup	2-1/4 cups
Shortening, softened	1/4 cup	3/4 cup
Egg	1	3
Milk	1/2 cup	1-1/2 cups
Flour, sifted	2 cups	6 cups
Baking Powder	2 tsp.	2 tbsp.
Salt	1/2 tsp.	1-1/2 tsp.
Blueberries, well drained	2 cups	6 cups
CRUMB MIXTURE		
Granulated Sugar	1/2 cup	1-1/2 cups
Flour, sifted	1/3 cup	1 cup
Cinnamon	1/2 tsp.	1-1/2 tsp.
Butter, softened	1/4 cup	3/4 cup

METHOD

1. Mix thoroughly the sugar, shortening, and egg.
2. Stir in milk.
3. Sift together flour, baking powder, and salt; stir into above mixture.
4. Carefully blend in blueberries.
5. Sprinkle top with Crumb Mixture made by mixing together sugar, flour, cinnamon, and butter.
6. Bake in oven at 375°F. for 45 to 50 minutes.
7. Serve with heavy cream, whipped cream, ice cream, or Lemon Sauce (recipe, p. 229)

★ See picture, facing page.

BLUEBERRY BUCKLE

North American
Blueberry
Council

Houston Club

Houston, Texas

The Houston Club was chartered in 1894 for "literary purposes; to promote social intercourse among its members, and to provide for them the convenience of a club house." Housed in an 18-story building in downtown Houston, the club occupies floors 7 through 10 and has 36 dining areas.

It was the first private club to receive a "First" award from *Institutions/VF* Magazine in its foodservice design competition. Realizing that good food and good foodservice start in the kitchen, the entire club is laid out around the kitchen. The club has won numerous awards for design and the effort to excel is reflected in the food served.

Houston Club

HOUSTON CLUB KIRSCH TORTE ★

(5 layers of toasted almond meringue layered with kirsch-flavored dark cherries and Grand Marnier whipped cream)

YIELD:	1 TORTE (12 PORTIONS)	2 TORTES (24 PORTIONS)
INGREDIENTS		
MERINGUE		
Egg Whites	1 pt.	1 qt.
Granulated Sugar	14 oz.	1 lb., 12 oz.
Confectioners' Sugar, sifted	1 lb.	2 lb.
Almonds, toasted, finely ground	1/2 lb.	1 lb.
FILLING		
Dark Sweet Cherries, Pitted	7 cups	1 No. 10 can
Kirsch	1/2 cup	1 cup
Grand Marnier	1/4 cup	1/2 cup
Heavy Cream	1 qt.	2 qt.
Vanilla	dash	dash
Confectioners' Sugar	1-1/4 cups	12 oz.
GLAZE		
Dark Sweet Cherry Juice, drained from	7 cups	1 No. 10 can
Granulated Sugar	1/2 cup	1/2 lb.
Kirsch-Grand Marnier Marinade plus Water	1 cup	2 cups
Gelatine, unflavored	2 oz. (2 packets)	4 oz.
Red Food Coloring	few drops	few drops

METHOD

1. Beat egg whites until soft peaks form. Add the granulated sugar a little at a time and continue beating on third speed to form a stiff meringue. Fold in the sifted confectioners' sugar and almonds.

★ See picture, page 86.

2. Use a pastry bag or a spoon to form ten 12-inch meringue layers on bun-pan-liner paper or brown paper.
3. Place in a warm location (on top of oven) to dry for 24 hours.
4. Remove paper.
5. To make filling, drain juice from cherries and save for Glaze.
6. Marinate the cherries for several hours or overnight in kirsch and Grand Marnier.
7. When ready to assemble, beat heavy cream until almost thick. Add confectioners' sugar and dash of vanilla and continue beating until thick.
8. Drain cherries well, reserving liqueurs used as a marinade.
9. For Glaze, to the drained cherry juice, add granulated sugar; bring to a boil.
10. Add drained kirsch-Grand Marnier marinade, gelatine, softened in marinade, and red food coloring.
11. Mix well and remove from heat.

To assemble Torte, place layer of meringue on tray. Spread with thin layer of whipped cream. Cover layer with cherries about 1-1/2 inches apart. Drizzle lightly with Glaze. Repeat until five layers of meringue have been used.

Using a No. 22 pastry tube, decorate the sides and top with whipped cream. Dip cherries in glaze and place decoratively on top. Tint remaining whipped cream a pale green and use leaf tip (No. 70) to form leaves next to cherries. If desired, sprinkle on shaved chocolate.

HOUSTON CLUB KIRSCH TORTE

India House

New York. New York

For centuries "India" and "The Indies" stood for all that was bold, alluring, and profitable in trade and adventure. "India House" is a fitting name for a club composed solely of executives engaged in maritime commerce (ship builders and owners, maritime insurors, or those who specialize in maritime commerce in their respective fields, such as banking and law).

The New York City club is located near the docks on lower Manhattan Island, a spot where the sea commerce of early New York was centered.

The home of India House was built in 1837, in the reconstruction following the great fire of 1835 which destroyed 600 buildings in the heart of New York's business district. (The building was declared a historical landmark 3 years ago.)

India House as an organization came into being in 1914 when a number of businessmen leased the building and decorated the rooms in the spirit of early American overseas trade. Ship models, engravings and oil paintings, art objects, maritime relics, and a large collection of artifacts related to foreign commerce and the sea contribute to the nautical emphasis of the decor.

STEAK AND KIDNEY PIE

(A crusty old English favorite made with oysters)

YIELD:	4 PORTIONS	24 PORTIONS
INGREDIENTS		
Lamb Kidneys	4	24
Beef, Lean, cut in 1-1/2 oz. pieces	1 lb.	6 lb.
Butter	1 oz.	6 oz.
Onion, finely chopped	1 to 2 oz.	6 oz.
Garlic, minced	1 clove	6 cloves
Flour	1 tbsp.	1/3 cup
Water *or* Beef Stock	1 pt.	3 qt.
Red Wine	1/2 cup	3 cups
Carrots, Small	4 to 8	24 to 48
Onions, Small	4 to 8	24 to 48
Green Peas	1 cup	6 cups
Mushrooms	1 cup	6 cups
Potatoes, Small, steamed	4 to 8	24 to 48
Fresh Oysters	4	24
Pie Crusts	4	24

METHOD

1. Wash lamb kidneys in cold water. Cut each into 4 pieces. Brown pieces of kidney and beef in butter.
2. Add onion and garlic; saute.
3. Stir in flour.
4. Add water or stock and red wine; simmer about 2-1/2 hours.
5. Place stew in baking dishes; add pre-cooked carrots, small onions, green peas, mushrooms, and tiny steamed potatoes. Top each portion with one fresh oyster and pie crust.
6. Bake in preheated oven at 350°F. for 25 to 30 minutes, or until crust is golden brown.

India House

INDIA HOUSE CLAM CAKES

(Not crab, but clam cakes—brown and crusty)

YIELD:	6 PORTIONS	24 PORTIONS	
INGREDIENTS			METHOD
Potatoes, Medium-Sized	3	12	1. Boil potatoes in jackets; peel and mash.
Onion, chopped	1	4	2. Saute the onion in butter. Add clams and
Butter	1/4 lb.	1 lb.	cook for 2 minutes.
Clams, shucked, chopped	3 cups	3 qt.	3. Add the remaining ingredients, together with the mashed potatoes, to the clams.
Clam Juice	1/4 cup	1 cup	4. Shape into flat cakes and pan-fry in moder-
Eggs	2	8	ately hot fat until crusty on both sides.
Celery Salt	to taste	to taste	Serve with Tomato, Dill, or Tartar Sauce.
Parsley, chopped	1 tsp.	1-1/2 tbsp.	
Celery Leaves, chopped	1/2 tsp.	2 tsp.	

INDIA HOUSE CURRY SAUCE

(An Indian specialty served with a vast array of condiments)

YIELD:	6 PORTIONS	24 PORTIONS	
INGREDIENTS			METHOD
Butter, melted	1/3 cup	12 oz.	1. In melted butter, saute onion, celery, and green pepper; stir in curry powder and flour.
Onion, chopped	1	4	
Celery, chopped	2 ribs	8 ribs	2. Gradually add chicken broth and cook slowly for 10 minutes.
Green Pepper, chopped	1/2	2	3. Add the tomato, apple, chutney, and coco-
Curry Powder	1 tbsp.	1/4 cup	nut; simmer about 35 minutes.
Flour	2 tsp.	2 tbsp. plus 2 tsp.	4. Season with salt to taste. Serve with cooked rice.
Chicken Broth	1 pint	2 qt.	5. Condiments to be served on tray accom-
Tomato, chopped	1	4	panying curries: Bombay duck, ground nut-
Green Apple, chopped	1	4	meg, chutney, raisins, shredded coconut, sliced egg, capers, smoked salmon, fried
Chutney	1 tbsp.	1/4 cup	onion rings, chopped chives, chopped pars-
Coconut	1 tbsp.	1/4 cup	ley, dill pickle slices.
Salt	to taste	to taste	

Interlachen Country Club

Edina, Minnesota

The visionaries who came out to the end of the Minneapolis streetcar line and bought three farms (paid for in gold and gold certificates) to start their country club would not recognize much externally about the club or Edina today. But many of their old mandates are continued in the kitchen.

Mixing wild rice with white rice is still a club "no-no"; the club feels it is not necessary as 2 ounces of wild rice, when cooked, will serve 11 to 12 people. Another "no-no" has to do with the cooking of wild rice. The preferred manner is to soak the kernels and let them swell, then simmer *only* 15 minutes in just enough water so the rice absorbs all of it.

Before serving, the rice is combined with a mixture of onion, bacon, and chicken base. The onion and bacon have been minced, then sauteed together with the chicken base.

The club's famous Wild Rice Croquettes are made by adding egg to a very heavy cream sauce and stirring in cooked wild rice. The croquettes are scooped out with an ice cream scoop, and an indentation is made with the thumb so that before the croquette goes into the hot fat it looks a bit like a doughnut. After coming from the fryer, the indentations are filled with currant jelly. The croquettes make an unusual and delicious garnish on a platter, particularly with wild game (good, too, with beef tenderloin), and they can be frozen.

Pheasant is never roasted at Interlachen. Instead it is boned, floured, and sauteed in butter with fresh mushroom slices. Then it is simmered, like swiss steak, in a sauce of Madeira wine and brown stock for 45 minutes. Sour cream is stirred in just before serving. Only breasts and thighs are served at dinner. The drumsticks are prepared using the same method and served for luncheon on a bed of pasta, rice, or wild rice.

MATJES HERRING IN TOMATO SAUCE

(A Scandinavian favorite)

YIELD:	1 POUND	4 POUNDS
INGREDIENTS		
Matjes Herring	3/4 lb.	3 lb.
Tomato Catsup	1/2 cup	2 cups
Granulated Sugar	1/4 cup	1 cup
Cider Vinegar	1/4 cup	1 cup
Salad Oil	1/4 cup	1 cup
Bermuda Onion, thinly sliced	1/4 cup	1 cup
Bay Leaf, broken	1	3 or 4
Salt	to taste	to taste
Pepper	to taste	to taste

METHOD
1. Cut herring into 1-inch pieces.
2. Combine all ingredients and mix by hand in a bowl. Add herring.

HONEY DRESSING FOR FRUIT SALADS

(Pink and pretty, this thick dressing is particularly good on orange or grapefruit salads)

YIELD:	2 CUPS	1 GALLON
INGREDIENTS		
Granulated Sugar	2-1/4 cups	8 lb.
Fresh Lemon Juice	1/4 cup	1 pt.
Pineapple Juice *or* Maraschino Cherry Juice	1/2 cup	1 qt.
Honey	1-1/2 cups	6 lb.
Celery Seed	1 tbsp.	1/2 cup
Red Food Coloring	as needed	as needed

METHOD
1. Combine sugar and juices; hold over hot water for at least 2 hours (sugar dissolves and sauce thickens during this time).
2. Add honey, celery seed, and red food coloring.
3. Chill thoroughly.

INDIVIDUAL SHERRY TRIFLES

(An elegant dessert—sherry-soaked macaroons topped with Trifle Custard and rum-sparked whipped cream-nestles in a champagne glass)

YIELD:	6 to 8 PORTIONS	24 to 30 PORTIONS
INGREDIENTS		
CUSTARD		
Eggs, separated	4	16
Granulated Sugar	4 oz. (1/2 cup)	16 oz. (2 cups)
Salt	pinch	1/4 tsp.
Cream Sherry *or* Madeira	3/4 cup	3 cups
Flour	1 tbsp.	1/4 cup
MACAROONS		
Almond Paste	1 lb.	4 lb.
Granulated Sugar	8 oz. (1 cup)	32 oz. (4 cups)
Confectioners' Sugar	8 oz. (1 cup)	32 oz.
Egg Whites	6	24

METHOD

1. In a double boiler, over hot water, cook together egg yolks, sugar, salt, and sherry or Madeira.
2. Stir constantly until custard thickens; work in flour.
3. Cook 2 minutes longer.
4. Cool custard and fold in stiffly beaten egg whites.
5. For macaroons, combine almond paste and sugar. Add enough egg white to slacken paste sufficiently to go through large pastry tube.
6. Individual macaroons should be the size of a 50-cent piece when placed on unglazed paper.
7. Bake in oven at 325°F. for 20 to 25 minutes.
8. Place 1 macaroon, soaked in cream sherry, in a champagne glass.
9. Fill glass with Trifle Custard and sprinkle with crumbled macaroons.
10. Top with whipped cream flavored with dark rum.

PECAN TORTE

(Pecan meringue layered with whipped cream and topped with home-made caramel sauce)

YIELD:	8 to 9 PORTIONS	15 to 18 PORTIONS
INGREDIENTS		
TORTE		
Eggs, separated	6	12
Granulated Sugar	1 cup	2 cups
Salt	pinch	pinch
Pecan Meats, broken	1/2 cup	1 cup
Soda Crackers, broken	1/2 cup	1 cup
Vanilla	to taste	to taste
Heavy Cream	1 cup	1 pt.
CARAMEL SAUCE		
Brown Sugar	1 pt.	1 qt.
Heavy Cream	1 pt.	1 qt.
Butter	1/4 lb.	1/2 lb.

METHOD

1. Beat egg yolks, sugar, and salt together until thick.
2. In a separate bowl, beat egg whites until stiff; fold into egg yolk mixture together with pecans, soda crackers, and vanilla.
3. Pour into 2 well-greased and lightly floured pie pans or, if making large amount, use a steam table pan and cut in half after baking.
4. Bake in oven at 375°F. for 30 minutes.
5. When cool, assemble 2 layers with whipped cream in the middle and on top.
6. Serve with Caramel Sauce.
7. Combine all sauce ingredients and boil together gently for 5 minutes.
8. Cool and serve.

Interlachen Country Club

The Kansas City Club

Kansas City, Missouri

Back in 1882 when the Kansas City Club first opened in 1 hotel room, rented so that friends might gather to smoke an evening cigar without polluting the atmosphere of their wives' sitting rooms, it subscribed to "all the leading English newspapers published in the world." The club is still very "worldly."

That single smoky room has grown to a gracious, 14-story clubhouse with some of the most beautiful ceilings to be found anywhere in clubdom. So handsomely designed was the original clubhouse that most of it has been left relatively unchanged since its opening in 1922 (an occasion for which 6 orchestras played and the club's kitchens served to 900 people a six-course dinner).

There is richly carved walnut paneling throughout the club and leaded glass windows of great elegance. The club's main banquet room is fittingly called the Tudor Room. The central portion of this great hall is 2 stories high with heavy oak supporting a balcony on 3 sides of the room. Smaller dining rooms open off the U-shaped promenade formed by the balcony. Here there are 12 stained glass windows.

Henry VIII would have felt at home with the club's massive, feudal elegant decor.

LOBSTER AMERICAINE

(Cognac and white wine flavor the sauce enhancing tender lobster)

INGREDIENTS	4 PORTIONS	24 PORTIONS
Lobster, 2 lbs.	4	24
Lobster Roe	4	24
Salt	1/2 tsp.	1 tsp.
Cayenne Pepper	1/8 tsp.	3/4 tsp.
Oil	2 tbsp.	3/4 cup
Butter	2 tbsp.	3/4 cup
Onion, chopped	1/2 cup	3 cups
Shallots, chopped	4	24
Garlic	1 clove	6 cloves
Thyme	1/4 tsp.	1-1/2 tsp.
Chervil	1/8 tsp.	3/4 tsp.
Cognac	2 tbsp.	3/4 cup
White Wine	1/2 cup	3 cups
Tomatoes, quartered	1	6
Brown Fish Stock (recipe, p. 235)	1/2 cup	3 cups
Butter	1 tbsp.	6 tbsp.
Cornstarch	1 tsp.	2 tbsp.
Parsley, chopped	1/4 cup	1-1/2 cups

METHOD

1. Cut lobster in half lengthwise and separate claws from bodies. Clean, saving the roe.
2. Season lobster halves with salt and cayenne pepper, then saute in oil until meat stiffens and shells turn red.
3. In butter, saute onion, shallots, and garlic together with crushed thyme and chervil. Flambe with cognac; add white wine, tomatoes, lobster halves, and fish stock. Cover and cook in oven at 350°F. for 18 to 20 minutes.
4. Remove lobster and reduce the sauce.
5. At the Kansas City Club the lobster meat is then separated from the shells and placed in special small copper casseroles. If no individual casseroles are available, the tail meat may be loosened and the meat in the claws removed and placed in front of the body on a plate.
6. Strain the roe and mix it with butter and cornstarch. Use this to thicken the reduced Lobster Sauce. Pour over lobster meat and garnish with chopped parsley.

The Kansas City Club

HOLLYWOOD CHICKEN PIE

(Chicken pie gone glamorous! Chicken, flambeed in cognac, nestles under a flaky puff paste crust together with sweetbreads, apple, and pineapple)

YIELD:	2 PORTIONS	20 PORTIONS
INGREDIENTS		
Fryer Chicken	1	10
Butter	3 tbsp.	1/2 lb. or as needed
Whiskey *or* Cognac	as needed	as needed
Sweetbreads	2 slices	20 slices
Chicken Livers	2	20
Apple, peeled, sliced	1/3	3
Pineapple, Fresh *or* Canned	1/2 slice	5 slices
Fond*		
Puff Paste		

METHOD
1. Cut chicken into 4 pieces and saute in butter for about 15 minutes. Remove bones and flambe the meat in whiskey or cognac.
2. Saute sweetbread slices and chicken livers in butter; then saute apple and pineapple slices.
3. Place all ingredients in a casserole, add some brown chicken fond, and cover with puff paste.
4. Bake in oven at 375°F. for 10 to 15 minutes.

*Fond is caramelized drippings deglazed (loosened from pan bottom with a small amount of liquid).

POTAGE EMERAUDE ★

(This can only be served in the spring as the peas are cooked in the pods before they are shelled)

YIELD:	2 QUARTS	5 GALLONS
INGREDIENTS		
Peas, in Pods	2 lb.	20 lb.
Iceberg Lettuce, chopped	1 head	10 heads
Fresh Spinach, chopped	1 lb.	10 lb.
Parsley, chopped	2 tbsp.	1-1/4 cups
Seasoning Salt	to taste	to taste
White Pepper	to taste	to taste
Chicken Stock	1 pt.	2-1/2 qt.
Heavy Cream	1/2 pt.	5 pt.
Egg Yolks	3	30
Chicken Breasts, cooked, diced	as needed	as needed

METHOD
1. Cut pods at both ends; cook peas together with lettuce, spinach, and parsley until mixture is very green in color. Drain.
2. Remove peas from pods. Put peas, pods, and other greens through a fine sieve (or use a blender, in which case it is not necessary to shell the peas).
3. Cook puree and chicken stock together for 10 minutes; skim. Add heavy cream and egg yolks.
4. To serve, place a small portion of diced chicken in each bowl and pour soup over it.
5. Garnish with chicken.

★ See picture, facing page.

POTAGE EMERAUDE

Western
Iceberg
Lettuce, Inc.

CREPES FROU FROU

(Nesselrode, sour cream, Grand Marnier, and walnuts combine to make these elegant crepes)

YIELD: 8 PORTIONS   24 PORTIONS

INGREDIENTS	8 PORTIONS	24 PORTIONS
CREPES		
Flour, sifted	1-1/2 cups	1 lb., 2 oz. (4-1/2 cups)
Sugar	1/4 cup	6 oz. (3/4 cup)
Eggs, beaten	3	9
Butter, melted	4 tbsp.	6 oz. (3/4 cup)
Milk	1 cup	3 cups
FILLING		
Nesselrode	1 can	3 cans
Thick Sour Cream	1-1/2 cups	4-1/2 cups
Lemon Juice	1 tbsp.	3 tbsp.
WHIPPED CREAM SAUCE		
Egg Yolks	6	18
Granulated Sugar	1/2 cup	12 oz. (1-1/2 cups)
Heavy Cream	1 cup	3 cups
Grand Marnier	to taste	to taste
Confectioners' Sugar	as needed	as needed
Walnuts, toasted, chopped	as needed	as needed

METHOD

1. For crepes, combine flour, sugar, and eggs.
2. Add melted butter, stirring to form a smooth paste.
3. Moisten paste gradually with milk to make a thin cream.
4. Pour into a heated skillet, rotating to make very thin pancakes.
5. To make filling, drain Nesselrode. For each crepe, fold 1 tsp. of Nesselrode into 8 tsp. thick sour cream to which has been added a few drops of lemon juice.
6. Fill crepes and place on a greased platter or plates to keep warm in oven.
7. For whipped cream sauce, beat together egg yolks and sugar in double boiler over hot water until eggs are thick and smooth; cool.
8. Whip cream to very stiff consistency. Fold cream into cooled egg mixture, adding a little Grand Marnier or other liqueur. Pour over filled crepes.
9. Brown each portion lightly under a salamander; sprinkle with confectioners' sugar and toasted walnuts.

Kona Kai Club

San Diego, California

Kona Kai means "trade winds" in the Hawaiian language, and the Kona Kai Club is located on a man-made peninsula in San Diego, only 10 minutes from the heart of the city. The clubhouse has stunning views of the water and the city and boasts a 150-boat marina with a walkway directly to the clubhouse, a private beach on the "cleanest harbour in the U. S.," tennis courts, handball courts, a pool, and all of the equipment necessary for playing in the sun and sea.

Californians not only love the sea, but also, according to the club's chef, they love all fish and seafood and would rather have it than any kind of meat. One of their favorites is Totuava, a fish native to the San Diego waters. It is described as "so good it does not even need to be sauced." The delicate fish is lightly floured, sauteed in butter, and quickly finished in the oven. It is served with Meuniere Butter and garnished with lemon and parsley.

Seafood salads are a particularly favorite way to enjoy the ocean's fare, and the club uses avocado in every seafood salad served. But the head chef is wise enough to leave preparation of that other avocado favorite, Guacamole, to the club's Mexican chefs.

SAN DIEGO GUACAMOLE ★

(the Mexican way to prepare Guacamole)

YIELD:	4 SALAD PORTIONS	25 SALAD PORTIONS
INGREDIENTS		
Avocados, Ripe, peeled	2	12
Tomato, Small, diced	1	6
Yellow Pimiento, Hot, diced	1 or less	6 or less
Onion, finely chopped	1 tsp.	2 tbsp.

METHOD

1. Coarsely mash avocado with fork; add tomato, pimiento, and onion.
2. To keep guacamole from darkening, place the stone of the avocado in the middle of mixture until it is served.
3. Serve with corn chips or other Mexican dishes.

CRAB LEGS AMBASSADEUR

(Mushrooms and crab legs in a creamy sauce—topped with a trifle of truffle)

YIELD:	4 PORTIONS
INGREDIENTS	
Mushrooms, finely chopped	1 lb.
Shallots, finely chopped	5
Butter	as needed
Salt	to taste
Pepper	to taste
Heavy Cream	1/2 cup
Crab Legs	12 to 16
Brandy	as needed
Creamy Fish Veloute (recipe, p. 225)	2-1/2 cups
Hollandaise Sauce (recipe, p. 226)	6 tbsp.
Heavy Cream	6 tbsp.
Truffle, thin slices	as needed

METHOD

1. Place mushrooms and shallots in skillet with a little butter, salt, and pepper; reduce until all water has evaporated Add 1/2 cup heavy cream and mix well.
2. Saute crab legs with a little butter; remove from pan and deglaze (loosen any brown material) with a touch of brandy.
3. Arrange crab legs on top of mushrooms and shallots.
4. Heat Creamy Fish Veloute and remove from heat.
5. Fold in Hollandaise and the 6 tbsp. heavy cream. Cover crab legs with this *glacage.*
6. Top with thin truffle slices and run under a salamander or broiler until golden brown.

★ See picture, facing page.

SAN DIEGO GUACAMOLE

CREPE BENGALE

(Curry flavors crab to fill tender crepes)

YIELD:	8 PORTIONS	24 PORTIONS	
INGREDIENTS			**METHOD**
CREPES			
Flour, sifted	3/4 cup	2-1/4 cups	1. Sift flour, salt, and baking powder together into a bowl.
Salt	1/2 tsp.	1-1/2 tsp.	
Baking Powder	1/2 tsp.	1-1/2 tsp.	2. Beat eggs and add milk and water. Make a well in the flour and add egg mixture; stir to combine. For best results let batter sit a few hours.
Eggs	2	6	
Milk	2/3 cup	2 cups	
Water	1/3 cup	1 cup	
CRAB FILLING			3. Heat a 5-inch skillet and grease with a few drops of oil. Pour a small amount of batter into skillet. Tilt to spread batter. Turn crepes when set and golden brown.
Dungeness *or*			
Snow Crab	1/2 lb.	1-1/2 lb.	
Clarified Butter	as needed	as needed	4. For filling, heat crabmeat slowly in a skillet with a little clarified butter. Sprinkle with curry powder and add cream sauce; heat gently. Fill crepes and cover with Glacage.
Curry Powder	1 tsp.	1 tbsp.	
Cream Sauce			
(recipe, p. 225)	4 tbsp.	3/4 cup	
GLACAGE			5. To make Glacage, combine 3 tbsp. whipped cream and 2 tbsp. Hollandaise for each 2 crepe portion. Cover crepes with Glacage and place under salamander until golden brown.
Heavy Cream,			
whipped	3/4 cup	2-1/4 cups	
Hollandaise Sauce			
(recipe, p. 226)	1 cup	3 cups	

Kona Kai Club

VEAL ESCALOPE VALDOSTANA

(Prosciutto and mozzarella cheese sandwiched between thin slices of veal, served with a sauce made of mushrooms, artichoke bottoms, fresh herbs, and white wine)

YIELD:	1 PORTION	24 PORTIONS
INGREDIENTS		
Prosciutto, thinly sliced	1 slice	24 slices
Mozzarella Cheese, thinly sliced	1 slice	24 slices
White Veal (preferably loin), thinly sliced	2 slices	48 slices
Flour	1 tbsp.	1-1/2 cups
Egg, beaten	1	8
Dry White Bread Crumbs	2 tbsp.	3 cups
Parmesan Cheese	1 tsp.	1/2 cup
Clarified Butter	1 tbsp.	1 cup
Veloute Sauce (recipe, p. 225)	3 tbsp.	4-1/2 cups
Garlic, chopped	1 clove	12 cloves
Shallot, chopped	1	24
Mushrooms, diced	2	48
Artichoke Bottom, diced	1	24
White Wine	1 tbsp.	1-1/2 cups
Fresh Basil, chopped	1/2 tsp.	1/4 cup
Fresh Parsley, chopped	1/2 tsp.	1/4 cup

METHOD

1. Sandwich prosciutto and cheese between veal slices and press together tightly on the edges.
2. Dip Escalope on both sides, first in flour, then in beaten egg, and last in bread crumbs mixed with Parmesan cheese. Press so that bread crumbs adhere to the meat; brown in butter.
3. Heat in oven at 350°F. for 10 minutes to further melt the cheese. Pour a little Veloute Sauce into a serving skillet and place veal on the sauce.
4. In the skillet used to brown the veal, saute garlic and shallot with butter, then add chopped mushrooms and artichoke bottom; deglaze (loosen any brown material) with white wine. Sprinkle mixture with basil and parsley and pour over the veal.

The Lansdowne Club

London, England

Before World War I, it was difficult for medical men and lawyers to join a good English club, because old members disliked the idea of rubbing shoulders with people who knew too much about their insides or their business affairs. Today there is scarcely any job, except possibly that of a gossip writer, that automatically bars one from membership.

The Lansdowne clubhouse is older than our country, a fact that was emphasized when the manager said, "Oh, by the way, the Treaty of Independence with the United States was drafted in that room behind you."

This historic room is now a writing room. It is charming—rather small, completely circular (the club calls it the "Round Room") with brick walls 2 ft. thick and 12-ft. high windows admitting light to the portrait of the first Marquis of Lansdowne which hangs over the fireplace. The ceiling is a dome, decorated with a painted frieze of classical figures. The room is not at all the stiff and stately space that one expects to house history.

Shortly after that year so important in American history, Lord Shelbourne was named the first Marquis of Lansdowne, and the house has been known by his title since that time. Incidentally, it was in this house, too, that John Priestley discovered oxygen.

At the time the house was built, it was in the country. It is now in the center of one of the most fashionable areas in London, located on Berkeley Square in Mayfair. Unfortunately, in the 1930s the Westminster City Council decided to drive a new street through Berkeley Square, forcing the truncation of the front of Lansdowne House. Away went all of the front rooms.

One of these, the "first drawing room," was moved in its entirety across the Atlantic Ocean and reconstructed in the Pennsylvania Museum of Art, Philadelphia. The original facade was taken down and carefully reconstructed across the front of the shortened dwelling.

PIGEON PIE

(Steak, ham, and boiled eggs nest with the pigeon under a puff paste crust)

YIELD:	6 PORTIONS	24 PORTIONS
INGREDIENTS		
Pigeons	2	8
Rump Steak	1 lb.	4 lb.
Ham *or* Lean Bacon	4 oz.	1 lb.
Eggs, hard-cooked	2	8
Salt	to taste	to taste
Pepper	to taste	to taste
Beef Stock	1-1/2 cups	6 cups
Puff Paste	for 1 pie	for 4 pies
Egg Yolk	1	2
Water, cold	as needed	as needed

METHOD

1. Cut each pigeon into 4 pieces; bone.
2. Slice beef into small, thin slices, ham into julienne strips, and eggs into sections or slices.
3. Layer these ingredients in a pie dish. Season well and pour in stock to fill the dish 3/4 full.
4. Cover with a sheet of puff paste and brush with egg yolk which has been combined with a small amount of cold water. Bake in oven at 425°F. until the paste has risen and set. Then bake at 325° to 350°F. for about an hour. Serve hot.

The Lansdowne Club

SUCKLING PIG — ENGLISH STYLE

(A famous British club tells how it prepares a traditional holiday food)

YIELD: 10 PORTIONS

INGREDIENTS		METHOD
Suckling Pig, Small	1	1. Choose a very white, small suckling pig (ask butcher to shave and clean).
Onions	3 lb.	
Bread, torn	1 lb.	2. Prepare forcemeat as follows: Bake onions in their skins; allow to cool. Peel and chop very fine. Mix well with remaining ingredients. Stuff pig with the forcemeat.
Beef Kidney Fat, minced	1 lb.	
Salt	1 tbsp.	
Pepper	1 tsp.	3. Sew up the belly.
Nutmeg	1/2 tsp.	4. Place the pig on a spit, baste with oil, and roast in the normal way.
Sage, finely chopped	1 tbsp.	
Eggs	2	

LANSDOWNE BEEF CURRY

(From the club where the agreement that ended the Revolutionary War was signed)

YIELD: 6 PORTIONS   24 PORTIONS

INGREDIENTS			METHOD
Onions, finely chopped	2	8	1. Saute onions and garlic in oil for 4 minutes. Add chili and curry powders and saute 4 more minutes. Add beef cubes and stir well. Add tomato paste and enough flour to thicken sauce. Cover tightly and simmer until beef is tender. Just before serving, add salt and lemon juice.
Garlic, finely minced	1 clove	4 cloves	
Cooking Oil	2 tbsp.	4 oz.	
Chili Powder	2 tsp.	1 tbsp.	
Curry Powder	2 tsp.	1 tbsp.	
Topside of Beef, cubed	1 lb.	4 lb.	2. The chef suggests that this be served with boiled rice, dessicated coconut (peeled and dried, it looks like rice), Bombay duck, chutney, and pompadum. Pompadum is a very thin, dry bread-like product used to garnish the curry (when placed on top it disintegrates). It can be procured at an Indian grocery store.
Tomato Paste	2 tbsp.	4 oz.	
Flour			
Salt	to taste	to taste	
Lemon Juice	1/2 tsp.	2 tsp.	

Los Angeles Club

Los Angeles, California

The Los Angeles Club goes to great lengths in staging parties, and the Los Angeles area, land of make-believe, provides an unusual source for props and people. For one party the club employed four 6-ft., 8-in. giants, each weighing more than 300 pounds, to shoulder a platform bearing two midgets, in chef's uniforms, who were carried around the room to signal the beginning of a gourmet meal.

At the same dinner, goldfish bearing sequined numbers served as table markers. During the fish course the two midgets, this time attired in fishermen's oilskins, were transported through the dining area by the giants; each fisherman had a goldfish on his fishing line.

While the Los Angeles Club does not feature goldfish on its menu, it does serve many other fine fresh fish and believes that the best sauce for any fish is mousseline. The Los Angeles Club mousseline formula calls for blending fresh hollandaise sauce with unsweetened whipped cream and a small amount of English mustard.

Small coconuts from Puerto Rico are the basis for another dish. The nuts are cut very near the top and the lids removed. The coconuts (with their liquid still inside) are placed in a casserole with white wine and clam broth. The dish is covered, placed in the oven, and steamed. When the coconut meat has cooked, the liquid is poured out and each coconut is stuffed with a seafood mixture of little bay shrimp and cardinal of lobster finished with mousseline sauce, shallots, and a bit of bay leaf crushed in the hand. It is said the oils in the hand help release the herb's flavor. A puff paste lid tops the coconut's opening, and the dish is served nestled in a napkin which has been folded lotus-fashion.

When the guest has enjoyed the seafood, the coconut meat is removed and eaten. Accompanied by cold asparagus or cold broccoli vinaigrette, it makes a delightful luncheon dish.

California fruits, in various guises, are favorites with Los Angeles Club members. Small fresh strawberry fritters called strawberry beignets make an elegant dessert.

Schweppes soda water is mixed with sifted all-purpose flour to make a soft paste. Cleaned and dried strawberries (or raspberries, kumquats, or bananas) are picked up with an oyster fork, rolled in the paste, and fried in deep fat. The browned beignets are then sprinkled with confectioners' sugar and nestled in a napkin to keep them warm for service. At their peak, the beignets are crusty and the fruit inside is fresh and firm.

The beignets can be served alone or with a custard sauce flavored with a liqueur. At the Los Angeles Club Elixir d'Anvers is used for flavor, although any good orange-flavored liqueur could be used.

A simpler Club dessert is called Orange Cognac. Sections of peeled California oranges are well chilled for 2 hours. Then the sections are arranged in glass serving dishes centered with confectioners' sugar. Guests dip their orange sections in Cognac and then in the sugar before eating.

STRAWBERRIES BRUXELLOISE

(Peaches, raspberries, and strawberries flavored with Grand Marnier, then topped with whipped cream and macaroon crumbs)

YIELD:	8 PORTIONS	24 PORTIONS
INGREDIENTS		
Raspberries	1 pt.	3 pt.
Peaches	2	6
Strawberries	3 pt.	9 pt.
Grand Marnier	1-1/2 tbsp.	1/4 cup
Heavy Cream, whipped	1 cup	3 cups
Orange Peel	2 tbsp.	1/3 cup
Lemon Peel	2 tbsp.	1/3 cup
Fruit Syrup, from Canned Fruits	1/2 cup	1-1/2 cup
Macaroons	8	24

METHOD

1. Puree raspberries.
2. Slice peaches and add to the raspberry puree. Slice and add 2/3 of the fresh strawberries.
3. Add Grand Marnier.
4. Allow to stand for 6 hours before serving.
5. When ready to serve, divide the fruit-puree mixture into compotes. Put a rosette of freshly whipped cream in the center, and float on this 1 large, long-stemmed fresh strawberry.
6. Make a julienne of orange and lemon peels and marinate in syrup of any canned fruit. Sprinkle well-drained peel on top of compotes and then sprinkle crushed macaroons over all.

Louisville Country Club

Louisville, Kentucky

The French have heavily accented the history of Louisville, Kentucky. The city, one of the first cities of the American West (settled in 1778 by General George Rogers Clark and his small army during the Revolution), was named in honor of King Louis XVI. The choice of that name was a tribute to assistance contributed by the French during the Revolutionary War.

Louisville's location on the Ohio River, the main artery of civilization moving from the seaboard states to the developing American West, made it an important river port and frontier town. French trappers and people of varied nationalities converged at Louisville, bringing their individual cultures. Their contributions are still discernible, both in the cuisine and the cultural life of the city.

One of the Louisville Country Club's imaginative Americanized recipes is a Beef-Shrimp Stroganoff. The dish does not contain mushrooms, but is otherwise made in the conventional stroganoff manner and served on a bed of wild rice. Shrimp are poached and used to garnish the dish, together with scoops of sour cream and sprigs of fresh parsley.

Another club creation, Veal Sea Scallopini, is made with large sea scallops poached in a combination of sauternes and sherry, and then sliced. The veal scallops are floured and sauteed, and a sauce is made with sherry and sliced, fresh mushrooms. The sea scallops and the veal scallops are combined with the sauce and served on a bed of green noodles.

STUFFED LEG OF LAMB

(A whole pork tenderloin encircled by tender lamb)

YIELD:	10 to 12 PORTIONS	20 to 24 PORTIONS
INGREDIENTS		
Leg of Lamb, boned	1(5-1/2 to 6 lb.)	2 (6 lb.)
Whole Pork Tenderloin	1 lb.	2 lb.
Seasoned Flour	as needed	
Garlic (optional)	2 cloves	4 cloves
French Dressing (recipe, p. 236)	1 cup	2 cups
Salt	to taste	to taste
Pepper	to taste	to taste
Flour	2 tbsp.	1/4 cup (2 oz.)
Stock *or* Water	2 cups	1 qt.

METHOD

1. Bone lamb and fill cavity with the pork, securing tightly with string. Save the bone and cook with the meat for flavor. Insert slivers of garlic in the lamb, if desired.
2. Marinate 2 hours in French Dressing. Rub with seasoned flour. Roast in oven at 350° F. for 3 hours, or until pork is well cooked. Transfer to hot platter and allow to rest for about 20 minutes before carving.
3. To make gravy, pour off fat from pan, blend in flour, add stock, and cook until thickened, stirring constantly.
4. At the Louisville Country Club this is served with eggplant paysan, chilled tomato slices, hot rolls, and molded creme amandine.

BEEF IN HORSERADISH SAUCE

(Sour cream, horseradish, and big chunks of tender beef make a beautiful stew)

YIELD:	8 PORTIONS	24 PORTIONS
INGREDIENTS		
Beef Stew Meat, cubed	3 lb.	9 lb.
Salt	2 tsp.	2 tbsp.
Pepper	1/2 tsp.	1-1/2 tsp.
Browned Flour*	1/3 cup	1 cup
Onions, chopped	2	6
Beef Bouillon or Stock	1 No. 1 can	30 ounces
Water or Wine	1/3 cup	1 cup
Worcestershire Sauce	1-1/2 tbsp.	4-1/2 tbsp.
Sour Cream	1-1/2 cups	4-1/2 cups
Prepared Horseradish	3 tbsp.	1/2 cup

METHOD

1. Season beef with salt and pepper, dust with flour, and place in a buttered casserole.
2. Top with onions and pour the stock, water, and Worcestershire sauce over all. Cover tightly and cook slowly in oven at 300°F. for 3 hours until the meat is very tender.
3. If necessary, reduce the sauce by boiling rapidly.
4. Just before serving, stir in the sour cream and horseradish. *Do not allow mixture to boil.*
5. At the Louisville Country Club this is served with toasted french bread, broccoli, and sherry torte.

*To brown flour, heat slowly in a medium oven or in a heavy skillet on top of the range, stirring frequently to prevent burning.

TURKISH VEAL STEW

(Middle Eastern spices and coconut make an exotic stew)

YIELD:	6 PORTIONS	24 PORTIONS
INGREDIENTS		
Veal Stew Meat	3 lb.	12 lb.
Veal Bones	as reserved	as reserved
Onions, Large, minced	2	8
Coconut, grated	1/4 cup	1 cup
Cinnamon	1/4 tsp.	1 tsp.
Thyme	1/4 tsp.	1 tsp.
Ground Cloves	1/4 tsp.	1 tsp.
Salt	2 tsp.	2-1/2 tbsp.
Pepper	1/2 tsp.	2 tsp.
Bay Leaf, crumbled	1	4
Tomatoes, peeled, sliced	3	12
Sauterne	1-1/2 cups	5-1/2 cups

METHOD

1. Cut veal into 1-1/2-inch cubes. Save the bones. Place meat in a non-metallic bowl.
2. Add all ingredients except tomatoes, wine, and bones. Mix well, cover, and let stand several hours.
3. Transfer to a buttered casserole. Add tomatoes and wine, topping with veal bones. Cover tightly, bring to boiling point, and cook slowly in the oven at 300°F. for 4 hours. Uncover the last hour of cooking time so that the liquid will reduce. Remove the veal bones before serving.
4. At the Louisville Country Club this is served with saffron rice, a mixed vegetable salad, and pineapple-lemon sherbet.

DERBY PIE

(A Kentucky pecan pie made with chocolate chips and flavored with bourbon)

YIELD:	1 PIE	3 PIES
INGREDIENTS		
Granulated Sugar	3/4 cup	2-1/4 cups
Brown Sugar	1/4 cup	3/4 cup
Flour	1 tbsp.	3 tbsp.
Pecans	1 cup	3 cups
Chocolate Chips	1 cup	3 cups
Eggs, beaten	4	12
Butter, melted	8 tbsp.	12 oz. (1-1/2 cups)
White Corn Syrup	1 cup	3 cups
Vanilla	1 tsp.	1 tbsp.
Bourbon (optional)	to taste	to taste
Pie Crust, 9-inch	1	3

METHOD

1. Combine dry ingredients; beat eggs and add with dry ingredients to melted butter. Add white corn syrup and vanilla and a little bourbon if desired.
2. Pour into unbaked crust and bake in oven at 350°F. for 45 minutes.

Maple Bluff Country Club

Madison, Wisconsin

If someone told you he could make boiled fish taste like lobster you would probably take the information with a large grain of salt. But a mass of salt is a part of the secret in the taste transformation, and apparently the fish "cum lobster" does not taste too salty.

Early Scandinavian settlers in Wisconsin brought with them the custom of boiling fish, potatoes, and onions together. All of these components were plentiful, so, when there was a crowd to feed, the ingredients were boiled together in a large pot outdoors.

The dish is still so popular in Wisconsin that merchants sell specially made 12-1/2-qt. aluminum kettles, each with a metal basket insert and a cover with adjustable vents for the big fish boils. Anyone can improvise with an insert basket of some sort and a lid left slightly ajar. The Maple Bluff Country Club finds the dish so popular that they do it often in the summer—much as the clubs located on the coasts do clam bakes.

Any large, soft-finned fish can be used. In Wisconsin, whitefish, lake trout, steelheads, and coho salmon are favorites. Clean the fish, then cross-section into steaks 1-1/2 in. thick. One pound of fish steak per person is the ration when only men are being served; one-half pound per person when catering to a mixed group.

The potatoes should be new and uniform in size to ensure even cooking. Do not peel potatoes; scrub well and cut a thin slice from each end. Two potatoes per man, one per woman, and a peeled onion per portion is the normal allotment.

About 30 minutes before serving time, put the potatoes and 8 qt. of water in the kettle. Leaving the vents open, cover the kettle and let water come to a boil.

Then add the onions and *1 cup* of salt, slowly. As soon as the water boils again, cook the potatoes for 20 minutes with the vents still open. (The vents apparently are never closed, so in an ordinary kettle the lid would be slightly ajar throughout the cooking process.)

At the end of 20 minutes, lower the metal basket, filled with fish steaks, into the boiling water. Slowly add *1 more cup of salt.* Cover the kettle again with the vents open, and cook the fish, potatoes, and onions at a rolling boil for 12 minutes.

The cooking time may vary 2 or 3 minutes either way, depending on the size of the potatoes and the type of fish. When the dish is properly cooked, a fork should penetrate easily to the heart of the potato, and the fish should flake nicely.

When the contents are done, drain the fish, potatoes, and onions and serve piping hot with melted butter, chopped parsley, and sliced lemon.

The "fish boil" is an unusual one-dish meal for a group of any size—simple to prepare indoors or out.

Maple Bluff Country Club

LITTLE WIENERS IN ORANGE SAUCE

(A tangy orange flavor goes well with wieners or smoked sausages)

YIELD: 16 PORTIONS   96 PORTIONS

INGREDIENTS			METHOD
Granulated Sugar	3 tbsp.	1 cup	1. Mix sugar, cornstarch, cloves, and cinnamon in saucepan or shallow chafing dish.
Cornstarch	1/2 tbsp.	3 tbsp.	2. Blend in orange juice and vinegar.
Whole Cloves	1	6	3. Cook over medium heat, stirring constantly, until thick.
Cinnamon	pinch	1/4 tsp.	4. Add the little sausages and cook slowly for 5 minutes, or until heated through. Keep warm over low heat in chafing dish.
Orange Juice	1/4 cup	1-1/2 cups	
Cider Vinegar	2 tsp.	1/4 cup	
Little Wieners *or* Cocktail Smoked Sausages	1 pkg.	6 pkg. (5-1/2 oz. each)	

FRANK AND SAUSAGE CHAFING DISH APPETIZERS

(Cocktail franks and small smoked sausages in a spicy sweet-sour pineapple sauce)

YIELD: 10 PORTIONS   25 PORTIONS

INGREDIENTS			METHOD
Chili Sauce	1 jar (12 oz.)	30 oz.	1. Combine and heat to simmering all ingredients except the frankfurters and sausages.
Crushed Pineapple	1/2 cup	1-1/4 cups	2. Add meats and keep hot in a chafing dish or over a candle warmer for serving.
Currant Jelly	1/2 cup	1-1/4 cups	
Brown Sugar	1-1/2 tbsp.	1/4 cup	
Cider Vinegar	1-1/2 tbsp.	1/4 cup	
Liquid Hot Pepper Seasoning	3 dashes	1 tsp.	
Worcestershire Sauce	1/2 tbsp.	1-1/2 tbsp.	
Cocktail Frankfurters	1 lb.	2-1/2 lb.	
Smoked Cocktail Sausages	10 oz.	1-1/2 lb.	

ZIPPY HOT SAUSAGE APPETIZERS

(A colorful cocktail party idea that could also be done using cocktail wieners)

YIELD:	15 to 30 PORTIONS	100 PORTIONS
INGREDIENTS		
Pork Sausage Links	1-1/2 lb.	8 lb.
Pineapple Chunks	1 can (13 oz.)	65 oz.
Brown Sugar	1/2 cup	2-1/2 cups
Cornstarch	2 tbsp.	2/3 cup
Salt	1/4 tsp.	1-1/4 tsp.
Vinegar *or* Lemon Juice	1/4 cup	1-1/4 cup
Green Pepper, cut into 3/4-inch pieces	1/2	2-1/2
Maraschino Cherries, drained	1/2 cup	2-1/2 cups

METHOD

1. Cook sausage links and cut into bite-sized pieces.
2. Drain syrup from pineapple into measuring cup and add water to make 1 cup.
3. Combine sugar, cornstarch, and salt in a small bowl; stir in half of the pineapple liquid.
4. Heat the remaining liquid with vinegar or lemon juice in blazer of chafing dish over direct heat.
5. Add sugar-cornstarch mixture, stirring constantly until mixture thickens, about 5 minutes.
6. Add remaining ingredients and sausage links. Place over hot water in chafing dish.

SHRIMP KWANTUNG WITH PEA PODS

(A colorful Chinese dish, low in calories)

YIELD:	5 PORTIONS	25 PORTIONS
INGREDIENTS		
Butter *or* Cooking Oil	1/4 cup	1-1/4 cups
Mushrooms, sliced	1-1/2 cups	8 cups
Scallions, cut in large chunks	1/4 cup	1-1/4 cups
Chinese Pea Pods (Snow Peas)	1-1/2 lb.	8 lb.
Celery, diagonally sliced	1/4 cup	1-1/4 cups
Pimiento, chopped	1/4 cup	1-1/4 cups
Green Pepper, cut in large squares	1/4 cup	1-1/4 cups
Pepper	1/8 tsp.	1/2 tsp.
Shrimp, cooked, shelled, deveined	3 cups	4 qt.
Chicken Stock	3/4 cup	3-1/2 cups
Soy Sauce	1/3 cup	1-2/3 cups
Cornstarch	2 tbsp.	1/2 cup plus 2 tbsp.
Dry White Wine	1/2 tbsp.	3 tbsp.

METHOD

1. Stir-fry first 8 ingredients together until vegetables are tender-crisp.
2. Mix together the remaining ingredients and add to vegetables; cook until sauce is clear.
3. Serve with rice.

CHICKEN BREASTS WITH SAUSAGE SAUCE

(Sausage, pecans, and sherry make an unusual sauce for poached chicken breasts)

YIELD:	8 PORTIONS	24 PORTIONS
INGREDIENTS		
Chicken Breasts, boned and skinned	8	24
Salt	to taste	to taste
Pepper	to taste	to taste
Chicken Stock *or* Broth	2 cups	6 cups
Pork Sausage	1/4 lb.	3/4 lb.
Onion, Medium-Sized, chopped	1	3
Brown Seasoning Sauce	1 tsp.	1 tbsp.
Flour	1 tbsp.	3 tbsp.
Pecans, whole or chopped	1/4 cup	3 oz. (3/4 cup)
Sherry	2 tbsp.	6 oz. (3/4 cup)

METHOD

1. Season the chicken breasts with salt and pepper and place in a saucepot, adding half of the chicken stock. Cover and simmer gently for 45 minutes, or until chicken is tender.
2. Cook sausage in a skillet until done. Remove to blender container. Saute the onion in the drippings.
3. Add onion, remaining stock, seasoning sauce, and flour to sausage and run in the blender until sauce is pureed. Heat sauce in a pan until thickened. Add nuts and sherry.
4. Serve over hot, cooked chicken breasts.

WISCONSIN CHEESE SAUCE

(Serve with baked potatoes or toast points, or thin and serve as a soup)

YIELD:	3 CUPS	1-1/2 GALLONS
INGREDIENTS		
Butter	2 tbsp.	8 oz. (1 cup)
Cheddar Cheese, Sharp, grated	1 lb.	8 lb.
Light Beer	1/2 cup	1 qt.
Egg, beaten	1	8
Salt	1/2 tsp.	4 tsp.
Dry Mustard	1/2 tsp.	4 tsp.
Cayenne Pepper	dash	1/4 tsp.
Worcestershire Sauce	1 tsp.	3 tbsp.

METHOD

1. Melt butter and cheese in a saucepan with the beer.
2. Add a bit of the hot liquid to the beaten egg; then stir egg into cheese mixture.
3. Add seasonings. Stir until slightly thickened. Serve hot.

Metairie Country Club

New Orleans, Louisiana

New Orleans is as much a way of life as it is a city—a gracious formula for living, garnished with good food. The Metairie Country Club, once an old plantation, was established in 1923. Three small, private dining rooms in the clubhouse are named after the trees found on the original plantation—the Oak, Elm, and Maple rooms.

One of the club's claims to fame is possession of the longest pewter bar in the United States. It was imported from Paris and complements a collection of antique pewter on the back bar.

Many of the foods served at this and other clubs in the area are seasoned with Gumbo File—a seasoning much used in Cajun cuisine. It is a mixture of herbs with a strong sassafras base. Commercial files are available, but any New Orleans chef worthy of the name, makes his own (or has his mother blend it).

Local customs are practiced reverently, and the club's New Year's Day Buffet always has cabbage on the menu. To the Cajun that means there will be greenbacks aplenty in the year to come. And black-eyed peas must be there, too, so that there will be an abundance of change in the pockets as the calendar flips over.

Both mean good luck, and no one can ever have too much of that.

CRAYFISH OR SHRIMP BISQUE

(A Creole soup served with shrimp or crayfish balls)

YIELD:	1 QUART	1 GALLON
INGREDIENTS		
Shrimp *or* Crayfish	1 lb.	4 lb.
Water	1 qt.	1 gal.
Onion	1 small	1 large
Celery	1/2 rib	2 ribs
Garlic	1 clove	4 cloves
Pickling Spice	1 tsp.	4 tsp.
Salt	1 tsp.	1 tbsp.
Red Pepper, Crushed	1/4 tsp.	1 tsp.
Rice, cooked	1 cup	4 cups

METHOD

1. Make stock by boiling crayfish or shrimp together with onion, celery, garlic, pickling spice, salt, and crushed red pepper; cook 5 minutes.
2. Remove crayfish or shrimp and strain stock. Add rice and simmer 30 minutes; press through a China cap or blend in a blender. Bisque will be slightly shiny because of the rice.
3. Put seafood through food chopper on medium grind. Add 1/5 to the bisque. Use the remainder to make shrimp or crayfish balls.

SHRIMP OR CRAYFISH BALLS

Shrimp, chopped	1-1/2 cups	6 cups
Garlic, minced	1/2 clove	1 large clove
Bread Crumbs *or*		
Matzoh Meal Crumbs	2 tbsp.	1/2 cup
Celery Salt	1/4 tsp.	1 tsp.
Gumbo File*	to taste	to taste
Egg	1/2	2
Fat for deep frying	2 cups	1 qt.

SHRIMP OR CRAYFISH BALLS

4. Combine shrimp or seafood with garlic, bread crumbs, celery salt, gumbo file, and egg. Shape into balls about the size of thumbnail (Swedish meatball size) and roll in additional crumbs. Cook balls in deep fat at 375°F. until a light, golden brown. Serve with hot Bisque.

*Gumbo file is a commercially available seasoning with a sassafras base commonly used in Creole cooking. If it is unobtainable in your area, substitute seasoning salt.

OYSTER STUFFING

(A spicy, herby, Southern stuffing for turkey or fish—so good members buy it by the quart to take home)

YIELD:	8 PORTIONS	80 PORTIONS
INGREDIENTS		
Oysters	1-2/3 cups	1 gal.
Liquor from Oysters and Light Chicken Stock to equal	1-2/3 cups	1 gal.
Celery	1/4 rib	2 ribs
Onion	1/2	4
Scallions	2	2 bunches
Parsley	4 sprigs	2 bunches
Bell Pepper	1/4	2
Butter	as needed	as needed
Bay Leaf	1/2	3
Sage	1/2 tsp.	1 tbsp.
Stale Bread, coarsely chopped	7 cups	4 to 5 gal.
Salt	to taste	to taste
Pepper	to taste	to taste
Flavor Enhancer	to taste	to taste
Ground Allspice	1/3 tsp.	1 tbsp.
Gumbo File*	1/3 tsp.	1 tbsp.
Worcestershire Sauce	1/3 tsp.	1 tbsp.

METHOD

1. Simmer the oysters in their own liquor and stock, covered, 10 to 15 minutes. Set aside.
2. Put the vegetables through a chopper until vegetables are very fine. Saute them in butter, together with the bay leaves and sage, until tender. Remove bay leaves.
3. Drain the oysters, saving the liquid. Cut the oysters in half so that there are no large chunks. Combine the oyster halves and vegetables with the remaining ingredients.
4. Add oyster liquor-stock mixture to moisten dressing. Pat into roasting pans rubbed with oil. Sprinkle bread crumbs on top. Bake, uncovered, in oven at 350 to 375°F. for about 1 hour. (The stuffing can be reconstituted with more oysters and stock if it becomes dry.)

*Gumbo file is a commercially available seasoning with a sassafras base commonly used in Creole cuisine.

CORN FRITTERS

(Fried, as you would a pancake, these cooked-to-order specialties are great with ham or bacon)

YIELD:	1 DOZEN	4 to 5 DOZEN
INGREDIENTS		
Corn, Whole Kernel	1 No. 2-1/2 can	1 No. 10 can
Milk	1 cup	1 qt.
Flour	as needed	as needed
Sugar	1-1/2 tsp.	2 tbsp.
Bacon Fat	6 tbsp.	2 6-oz. ladles
Salt	to taste	to taste
White Pepper	to taste	to taste
Baking Powder	1 tbsp.	1/4 cup

METHOD

1. Grind all but 1/4 of the can of whole kernel corn, liquid and all.
2. Combine the ground corn with the reserved whole kernel corn. Add the remaining ingredients, using just enough flour to make the batter the consistency of pancake batter.
3. Fry in a well-greased frying pan on range (they are not deep fried). The batter should ooze off the spoon and flatten out in the pan. Cooked fritters should be oval shape, about 1 inch thick.

Metairie Country Club

Mid-America Club

Chicago, Illinois

Mid-America is definitely not a "clubbish" club with overstuffed leather chairs, a library, and well-aged members. Instead, it is a modern, classic, glass and chrome establishment located in a skyscraper high above Chicago's lakefront and skyline. The Mid-America Club is essentially a first class restaurant that is a private club . . . with one of the best wine cellars to be found anywhere.

To accommodate the club's basic membership—executives in Chicago's loop and Gold Coast areas who have neither the time nor the calories to spare for cooked-to-order, well-sauced entrees—the luncheon menu is a combination of French and American dishes. The dinner menu is entirely French.

Through contacts made by the many people on the club's staff who are of French birth and training, the club has been able to secure recipes for dishes that some of the most famous restaurants in France and other countries in Europe are noted for. Credit is always given to the establishments whose recipes are used, and as a consequence, feedback for those restaurants has developed in that Mid-America members traveling abroad make an effort to visit the birthplace of the dishes they have come to admire.

LOBSTER THERMIDOR

(White wine, Hollandaise, and seasonings gently flavor lobster meat before it goes back in its shell)

YIELD:	2 to 4 PORTIONS	24 PORTIONS
INGREDIENTS		
Maine Chicken Lobsters, Live	2 (1 lb. each)	24 (1 lb. each)
Butter	2 tbsp.	1-1/2 cups (3/4 lb.)
Mushrooms, finely chopped	1 cup	3 lb.
Shallot, finely chopped	1	8
English Mustard	1 tsp.	3 tbsp.
White Wine	1/4 cup	2 cups
Heavy Cream	1/2 cup	1 qt.
Salt	to taste	to taste
Cornstarch	1 tsp.	3 tbsp.
Cold Water	1 tbsp.	1/2 cup
Fresh Tarragon, Parsley, Chives	2 tsp.	1/3 cup
OR		
Dried Tarragon, Parsley, Chives	1 tsp.	3 tbsp.
Dijon Mustard	2 tsp.	1/3 cup
Hollandaise Sauce (recipe, p. 226)	1/2 cup	1 qt.
Heavy Cream, whipped	1/2 cup	1 qt.
Parmesan Cheese, grated	4 tsp.	1/3 cup

METHOD

1. Boil the live lobster in salted water for 25 minutes; remove meat from shell and chop.
2. Melt the butter in a heavy saucepan; add mushrooms; saute for 1 or 2 minutes.
3. Add chopped shallot, then the lobster meat; sprinkle with English mustard.
4. Add white wine; let it reduce a little. Add the cream, simmer down to one-third; then add salt and cornstarch combined with water; boil for a few seconds.
5. Add the chopped herbs, then the Dijon mustard; remove from heat immediately.
6. Add enough Hollandaise sauce combined with whipped cream to bind.
7. Spoon the mixture into the lobster shell halves; cover with remaining sauce; sprinkle with grated Parmesan cheese.
8. Glaze under broiler.

BREAST OF CHICKEN TRAVIATA ★

(Prosciutto and Swiss cheese nestled inside chicken breasts and served with a fresh mushroom-tomato sauce)

YIELD:	6 PORTIONS	24 PORTIONS
INGREDIENTS		
Chicken Breasts (4 to 5-1/2 oz. each)	6	24
Virginia *or* Prosciutto Ham	12 thin slices	48 thin slices
Swiss Cheese (sticks the size of golf pencils)	12 sticks	48 sticks
Oil	1 tbsp.	1/4 cup
Butter	2 tbsp.	1/2 cup
Salt	2 tsp.	2 tbsp.
White Pepper	1 tsp.	4 tsp.
Flour	as needed	as needed
Fresh Mushrooms, sliced	1/2 lb.	2 lb.
Tomatoes, Stewed	1 cup	32 oz. (4 cups)
Shallots, finely chopped	3	12
Dry White Wine	2 cups	2 qt.
Heavy Cream	2 cups	2 qt.
Brandy	3 tbsp.	6 oz. (3/4 cup)
Chives, chopped	1 tbsp.	1/4 cup
Hollandaise Sauce (recipe, p. 226)	1 cup	1 qt.

METHOD

1. Pound breasts of chicken until they become very thin. Divide each into 2 equal parts by cutting along center.
2. Wrap cheese sticks in ham and place 1 stick in center of each halved chicken breast. Fold each breast around ham-covered cheese, making certain every opening is closed tightly. Place in refrigerator for a few minutes to chill. (This preparation can be done a day in advance.)
3. One-half hour before serving, warm frying pans. Pour oil and butter into each pan. Season chicken breasts with salt and pepper and roll them in flour. When butter is melted, place chicken breasts in 1 pan and cook over low heat.
4. Place mushrooms in other pan and saute, keeping them moist and as uncolored as possible. Add finely chopped shallots and stewed tomatoes, letting them come to a boil; continue to simmer for a few seconds. Add wine and simmer until mixture has been reduced to about half. Add the cream and heat but do not simmer. Season to taste. Add brandy and remove from heat. Add chives and Hollandaise Sauce.
5. Keep chicken and sauce warm in a bain-maire or on top of opened oven door until serving time. *Be sure not to let the sauce boil again as the Hollandaise will break down and curdle.*

★ See picture, facing page.

BREAST OF CHICKEN TRAVIATA

Castle
and Cooke
Foods, Inc.

QUENELLES OF PIKE

(Light and lovely fish dumplings poached in white wine and fish stock)

YIELD: 8 PORTIONS

INGREDIENTS
Water	1 cup
Butter	4 tbsp.
Salt	1 tsp.
Flour, sifted	1 cup
Eggs	6 to 8
Fish Fillets, skinless, boneless	1-1/4 lb.
Beef Marrow *or* Suet	8 oz.
Nutmeg	pinch
Salt	1 tsp.
White Pepper	1/4 tsp.
Heavy Cream	1 to 2 cups
Truffles, chopped (optional)	2 tbsp.

METHOD

PREPARATION OF QUENELLE PASTE

1. The first step is making a pate a choux, which can be done a day early. Cover with waxed paper and store in the refrigerator.
2. Put the cup of water with the 4 tbsp. of butter and 1 tsp. of salt in a saucepan. When the water has come to a boil and the butter is fully melted, remove the pan from the stove and beat in the sifted flour, all at one time, mixing the ingredients with a wooden spoon or spatula.
3. Place the paste back on the stove over moderate heat for 2 or 3 minutes until the mixture forms a mass which does not stick to the pan or to your fingers.
4. Remove from stove and continue to beat until cooled. Then, one by one, add 3 to 4 eggs. Let mixture stand aside so that it may cool completely.
5. The second step is to force the fish fillets 3 times through a grinder equipped with a fine mesh sieve and place the ground fish in the refrigerator for a
6. Then grind the marrow or suet, once only.
7. Place the ground fish and marrow (or suet) in the bowl of an electric mixer and thoroughly mix it with a pastry blending attachment. Add 1 tsp. of salt, 1/4 tsp. of white pepper, a pinch of nutmeg, the chopped truffles, and 3 whole eggs. Continue to mix well for a few minutes.
8. Add 1 cup of the *pate a chou;* mix again for a few minutes, then slowly add the heavy cream, using 1 to 2 cups, according to how soft, fluffy, and light you prefer the quenelles.

SHAPING AND POACHING QUENELLES

9. There are several ways to shape the quenelles. The two most popular are (a) to roll them into

QUENELLES OF PIKE (Cont.)

cylindrical-shaped units on a floured board or (b) to employ the spoon methods whereby the quenelles are poached directly as you make them, similar to making any kind of dumpling.

10. The recommended procedure, however, is to shape the quenelles and arrange them in a buttered skillet or pan. After doing so, the boiling cooking liquid is poured over the quenelles and simmered 3 to 5 minutes. The liquid can be just salted water enriched with 1 cup of dry white wine, fish stock, or COURT BOUILLON.

PREPARATION OF COURT BOUILLON

11. Slice 1 carrot, 1 onion, 1 rib of celery; simmer together in a saucepan with 2 tablespoons butter.
12. Add 1 cup of white wine and let it reduce to half.
13. Add 5 cups of water, 1 tsp. salt, 1 bay leaf, a pinch of thyme, and 1 clove.
14. Let the bouillon simmer for 20 minuts.
15. Strain it and pour over the quenelles.

SHRIMP BOMBAY

(Shrimp the Asian way with a hint of curry and tomato)

YIELD:	8 PORTIONS	24 PORTIONS
INGREDIENTS		
Butter	1 tbsp.	3 tbsp. (1-1/2 oz.)
Shrimp, Jumbo-Sized, shelled, deveined, cooked	32 to 40	96 to 120
Curry Powder	2 to 3 tsp.	2 to 3 tbsp.
Heavy Cream	2 cups	6 cups
Catsup	2 to 3 tbsp.	1/2 cup (8 oz.)
Cornstarch	2 tsp.	2 tbsp.
Water	2 tbsp.	1/3 cup
Salt	to taste	to taste

METHOD

1. Melt butter in a heavy-bottomed saucepan; add shrimp and sprinkle with 2 to 3 tsp. curry, according to how strong the curry powder is.
2. Mix well and allow curry to melt in butter.
3. Add cream and catsup; bring to boil for a few minutes; stir in cornstarch combined with water; bring to boil. Add salt to taste.
4. Serve with white rice or toast, or both.
5. On the side may be served Pomapdom and Bombay duck (commercial products from India), kumquats, diced apples, orange rind, and shredded coconut.

The Minnesota Club

St. Paul, Minnesota

The Minnesota Club was organized in 1874, back when the surrounding woods were filled with Indians and traders. Like most cities, St. Paul has stretched and grown and shifted its principal parts. The central core of the city has slipped away from the beautiful, old clubhouse, but the new St. Paul Civic Center has grown up next door.

The proximity of the Civic Center has led to the design of special, limited, quick-service menus for theatre and hockey evenings.

Though the club building has been enlarged 3 times, great pains have been taken to keep the dining room identical to the original dining room. Construction details have been faithfully reproduced. Even the molds used in forming designs in the original plaster ceiling were copied in order to duplicate the old patterns in new plaster as the rooms grew in size.

SUPERB BARBECUE SALAD ★

(A colorful combination featuring watercress, romaine, cauliflower, almonds, avocado, and tomatoes in a tangy dressing)

YIELD:	4 PORTIONS	24 PORTIONS
INGREDIENTS		
Garlic, peeled, sliced	1 clove	6 cloves
Salt	1 tsp.	2 tbsp.
Lemon Juice	2 tbsp.	3/4 cup
Granulated Sugar	1/4 tsp.	1-1/2 tsp.
Black Pepper, Ground	1/4 tsp.	1-1/2 tsp.
Celery Seed	1/8 tsp.	3/4 tsp.
Paprika	1/2 tsp.	1 tbsp.
Dry Mustard	3/4 tsp.	1-1/2 tbsp.
Salad Oil	1/3 cup	2 cups
Lettuce	1 head	6 heads
Watercress	1 bunch	6 bunches
OR		
Romaine	1/2 bunch	3 bunches
Almonds, Blanched, Sliced, toasted	1/2 cup	3 cups
Cauliflower, florets	3/4 cup	4-1/2 cups
Garlic, peeled	1/2 clove	3 cloves
Avocado, Ripe, cut in pieces	1/2	3
Tomato, sliced, peeled	1	6

METHOD

1. Hours or days before serving, mash garlic with salt and lemon juice. Blend in the next 6 ingredients then add oil. Pour into a jar, shake well, and chill.
2. Early in the day salad is to be served, wash lettuce and watercress (or romaine); dry and tear. Prepare almonds and cauliflower.
3. Before serving, rub salad bowl well with peeled garlic clove. Fill bowl with greens, cauliflower florets, almonds, avocado, and tomato. Add dressing and toss.

★ See picture, p. 132.

SUPERB BARBECUE SALAD

The California
Avocado Advisory
Board

ORIENTAL BEEF-TOMATO

(A pan-stirred dish that is quickly made)

YIELD:	8 PORTIONS	24 PORTIONS
INGREDIENTS		
Sirloin of Beef *or*		
Rib Eye	2 lb.	6 lb.
MARINADE		
Fresh Ginger Root,		
minced	3 tbsp.	1/2 cup
OR		
Dried Ginger	1 tbsp.	3 tbsp.
Soy Sauce	1 cup	3 cups
Stock *or* Water	1/2 cup	1-1/2 cups
Granulated Sugar	3 tbsp.	1/2 cup
VEGETABLES		
Salad Oil *or* Shortening	1/4 cup	6 oz.
Onions, Small,		
cut in wedges	4	2 lb.
Scallions, cut in		
1-inch pieces	8	1 lb.
Celery, cut in 1-inch		
diagonal pieces	4 ribs	2 lb.
Green Peppers, cut		
in 1-inch squares	2	6
Tomatoes, cut in		
wedges	4	12
SAUCE		
Cornstarch	1/4 cup	6 oz.
Granulated Sugar	3 tbsp.	4 oz.
Broth *or* Water	1 pt.	3 pt.
Soy Sauce	1/2 cup	1-1/2 cups
Salt	1/2 tbsp.	1-1/2 tbsp.
Flavor Enhancer	1/2 tsp.	1-1/2 tsp.

METHOD

1. Cut meat into thin strips.
2. Combine marinade ingredients and marinate meat for 15 minutes.
3. Cut up vegetables, separating white and green portions of the scallions.
4. Remove meat from marinade; drain and saute in hot oil for only 15 minutes. Remove meat from pan and saute onions, white part of scallions, celery, and green peppers for about 5 minutes.
5. Combine ingredients for sauce and cook until thick. Add sauce to beef and vegetables.
6. Add tomatoes and tops of scallions. Heat and serve.

CHEF OWENS' KOLDOMAS

(Rice and beef-filled rolled cabbage baked in a tomato sauce)

YIELD:	6 PORTIONS	24 PORTIONS
INGREDIENTS		
Ground Beef	1 lb.	4 lb.
Egg	1	4
Rice, Uncooked	1/4 cup	1 cup
Onion, grated	to taste	to taste
Salt	to taste	to taste
Pepper	to taste	to taste
Milk	as needed	as needed
Cabbage	1 head	4 heads
Tomatoes	1 No. 2-1/2 can (3-1/2 cups)	1 No. 10 can
Salt	1 tsp.	1 tbsp.
Sugar	1 tsp.	1 tbsp.
Butter	1 tbsp.	3 tbsp.
Cornstarch	2 tbsp.	1/2 cup

METHOD

1. Combine ground beef, egg, rice, onion, salt, pepper, and enough milk to make a meatball consistency.
2. Core and parboil the entire head of cabbage. Separate cooked cabbage leaves. Roll beef mixture into cabbage leaves. Place in a baking pan.
3. Combine tomatoes, salt, sugar, and butter. Thicken with cornstarch blended with a little water until smooth. Bring to a boil and pour over meat-stuffed cabbage rolls.
4. Bake in oven at 350°F. for 1 hour.

The Minnesota Club

BRAISED BEEF WITH MUSHROOMS EN CASSEROLE
(Serve on buttered noodles in individual casseroles)

YIELD: INGREDIENTS	6 PORTIONS	25 PORTIONS
Beef Trim *or* Tips, cut in 1-inch cubes	3 lb.	12 lb.
Shortening	1/4 lb.	1 lb.
Garlic, minced	1/2 clove	2 cloves
Onion, thinly sliced	1/2 lb.	2 lb.
Salt	2 tsp.	2-1/2 tbsp.
Mushrooms, sliced	3/4 lb.	3 lb.
Tomato Paste	3 oz.	12 oz.
Beef Stock	6 cups	1-1/2 gal.
Flour	1 cup	1 lb.
Salt	to taste	to taste
Pepper	to taste	to taste

METHOD

1. Braise meat in shortening in oven at 375°F.; add garlic, onion, and salt. Cook until onion is transparent. Add mushrooms and tomato paste; cook 15 minutes longer. Add beef stock and cook 1 hour. Remove from oven. Drain stock from meat; strain stock and skim off fat, saving fat for the roux.
2. Make a roux by combining equal amounts of fat and flour. Add a small amount of roux to the stock to make a thin sauce. Gradually add more roux and cook until of medium consistency. Add meat combined with other ingredients. Simmer until meat is tender. Taste for seasoning.

CRABMEAT DELIGHT
(Thin pasta serves as a base for crabmeat, asparagus, and mushrooms in a cheese sauce; more cheese is sprinkled over all, then it goes into the oven)

YIELD: INGREDIENTS	4 to 6 PORTIONS	24 PORTIONS
Noodles, thin, broken	2 oz.	12 oz.
Cheese Sauce (recipe, p. 237)	1 cup	1-1/2 qt.
Cheddar Cheese, grated	1/4 cup	1/4 lb. (1 cup)
Crabmeat	4 oz.	24 oz.
Asparagus Tips, cooked*	8 to 12	72
Mushrooms, Medium-Sized, sliced, sauteed	4 to 6	1 lb.

*Frozen asparagus may be used.

METHOD

1. Cook noodles in boiling, salted water until slightly underdone, about 6 minutes; drain and place in buttered individual ramekins.
2. Arrange crabmeat, asparagus tips, and sliced mushrooms over noodles.
3. Cover with sauce; sprinkle with grated cheese.
4. Bake in oven at 350°F. for about 30 minutes.

INDIVIDUAL ORANGE SOUFFLES

(Inexpensive yet glamorous—a light and airy dessert)

YIELD:	6 PORTIONS	24 PORTIONS
INGREDIENTS		
Bread Crumbs, fine	1/2 lb.	2 lb.
Orange, grated rind and juice from	1	4
Milk	1 pt.	2 qt.
Granulated Sugar	3/4 cup	20 oz.
Butter	1/4 cup	8 oz. (1 cup)
Eggs, separated	4	16
Confectioners' Sugar	as needed	as needed

METHOD

1. Combine bread crumbs with grated orange rind in a large bowl.
2. Bring milk and sugar to just below boiling point; stir in the crumbs and add the butter. Allow to cool.
3. Add the orange juice and the beaten egg yolks.
4. Fold in stiffly beaten egg whites.
5. Pour into buttered individual souffle dishes or into buttered oven-proof coffee cups.
6. Bake in a preheated oven at 375°F. for 70 minutes. Dust with confectioners' sugar. Serve at once.

Missouri Athletic Club

St. Louis, Missouri

The chef at this club feels that chefs who keep their prize recipes tucked under their tall hats hold back the advancement of the culinary field. He believes in sharing and has more than 1,500 recipes in his files—all available to the kitchen crew of 64 who prepare the fare for the 16 private dining rooms and 4 public rooms where food is served in the club.

The staff bakes all of the club's pastries, breads, and rolls, including the myriads of tiny caramel rolls served at each meal.

One of the club's specialties, Riverboats Jean Laffite, does not require any cooking at all; it is a spoon or sip dessert which the club serves in a Cognac snifter. Here are the chef's directions: Pour 1-1/2 oz. (3 tbsp.) of Cognac into the glass. Ladle 1 scoop (No. 20) of chocolate ice cream into the glass and then place a spoon in with the cold ice cream (theoretically to keep the glass from breaking) while you *slowly* pour 1 scant cup of hot coffee over all. Twirl the spoon two times and serve at once.

AVOCADO BALLS WITH PASTA AND PISTACHIOS ★

(Spaghetti in a creamy, sherried casserole garnished with avocado balls)

YIELD:	8 PORTIONS	24 PORTIONS
INGREDIENTS		
Cornstarch	2 tbsp.	1/3 cup
Coffee Cream	1 cup	3 cups
Chicken Broth	1 cup	3 cups
Salt	1/2 tsp.	1-1/2 tsp.
White Pepper	1/4 tsp.	3/4 tsp.
Nutmeg	1/4 tsp.	3/4 tsp.
Turmeric	1 tsp.	1 tbsp.
Chicken Breasts, simmered, diced	2	6
Sherry	1/3 cup	1 cup
Spaghetti, cooked	12 oz.	2-1/4 lb.
Avocado Balls	1 cup	3 cups
Pistachio Nuts	1/4 cup	3/4 cup

METHOD
1. Blend cornstarch with cream; combine with chicken broth. Add seasonings and simmer until sauce is thickened; add chicken.
2. Just before serving, add sherry.
3. Serve in casserole with spaghetti; garnish with avocado balls and pistachio nuts.

YALANTZI DOLMA

(A delightful Greek appetizer to serve hot or cold)

YIELD:	10	30
INGREDIENTS		
Onion, finely chopped	1/3 cup	1 cup
Olive Oil	2 tbsp	6 tbsp.
Rice, Uncooked	1/2 cup	1-1/2 cups
Water	1/4 cup	3/4 cup
Salt	1/2 tsp.	1-1/2 tsp.
Pepper	1/8 tsp.	1/4 tsp.
Pine Nuts	2 tsp.	2 tbsp.
Currants	2 tsp.	2 tbsp.
Grape Leaves	10	30
Water, cold	2 tsp.	2 tbsp.
Lemon Juice	1 tsp.	1 tbsp.

METHOD
1. Saute onion in olive oil. Add rice. Then add remaining ingredients except cold water and lemon juice; cook until the rice is tender and starchy flavor is gone.
2. Spread grape leaf dull side down on a flat plate. Place 1 tbsp. of stuffing on center of each leaf and then, one at a time, fold over each of the sides to enclose. Fold the stem end over and roll leaf gently, but firmly, into a cylinder. Place in casserole, add cold water, and squeeze lemon juice over dolmas.
3. Cover and heat in oven at 350°F. for 15 minutes.

★ See picture, facing page.

AVOCADO BALLS WITH PASTA AND PISTACHIOS

The California
Avocado Advisory
Board

New Orleans Country Club

New Orleans, Louisiana

End-of-the-party breakfasts are an established New Orleans custom, and they usually consist of Grillades (veal cutlets or round steak cooked with tomato paste and Burgundy wine), grits, scrambled eggs, and bacon.

Another notable custom was the serving of red beans and rice every Monday, when the household help came in to do the washing and ironing. Today the dish is considered a treat any day of the week. The red beans of New Orleans are different from those found in the North, but any red bean is acceptable—particularly if you are not accustomed to the southern variety.

Some of the spices and seasonings used in Creole cooking are harder to substitute. One popular product is Rex Crab Boil, which comes packaged like tea bags, ready to put into the water with any kind of seafood. One good sniff and you sneeze on "forever."

Crayfish are used in almost all seafood dishes, and the club's Turtle Soup is locally famous. PoBoy sandwiches are a club favorite, but here they are chiefly of deep-fried oysters or shrimp.

One of the club's desserts is called the Triple "C" Pie. It is put together by covering a baked pastry shell with banana slices, then pouring in a layer of caramelized condensed milk, made by covering the milk can with water and simmering for 3 hours or more. Before serving, the caramel is topped with whipped cream flavored with a bit of rum or bourbon. Chopped pecans or pistachio nuts are sprinkled over all. Pistachio nuts are prettiest but pecans are favored—they are traditional.

GRILLADES

(This breakfast or midnight feast favorite is traditionally served with scrambled eggs)

YIELD:	6 PORTIONS	24 PORTIONS
INGREDIENTS		
Veal Cutlet		
or		
Round Steak, cut 3/4 inch thick	1-1/2 lb.	6 lb.
Salt	to taste	to taste
Pepper	to taste	to taste
Onion, thinly sliced	1	4
Garlic, minced	1 clove	4 cloves
Lard	as needed	as needed
Tomato Paste	1 can (6 oz.)	4 cans (6 oz.)
Water	2 cups	8 cups
Burgundy	1/2 cup	2 cups
Parsley	to garnish	to garnish

METHOD
1. Cut meat into 6 portions. Season with salt and pepper, rubbing seasoning in well.
2. Saute onion and garlic in lard until golden. Add tomato paste and water; stir well; add meat. Cover and cook slowly, turning occasionally until tender.
3. Add wine and simmer for 5 minutes.
4. Serve garnished with parsley.

TROUT TEODORA

(Gently garlicked crabmeat and shrimp in sauterne add greater glory to broiled trout)

YIELD:	4 PORTIONS	24 PORTIONS
INGREDIENTS		
Trout	4	24
Garlic, Large, finely minced	1 clove	6 cloves
Butter	1/4 cup	1-1/2 cups
Shrimp, cooked, medium chopped	1/2 cup	3 cups
Crabmeat	1/4 cup	1-1/2 cups
Salt	to taste	to taste
White Pepper	to taste	to taste
Flavor Enhancer	to taste	to taste
Sauterne	1/2 cup	3 cups

METHOD
1. Broil trout. Saute garlic in butter until a light brown; add shrimp, crabmeat, and seasonings.
2. Stir in wine and serve over broiled trout.

OYSTER STUFFING

(A Louisiana corn bread stuffing to serve with poultry or fish)

YIELD: 16 PORTIONS

INGREDIENTS		METHOD
Butter	8 tbsp. (1/4 lb.)	1. Melt butter and add celery, peppers, scallions, parsley, and garlic. Cook until vegetables are soft.
Celery, medium chopped	1 cup	2. Add oysters and giblets.
Bell Peppers, medium chopped	2 small	3. Pour over corn bread crumbs.
Scallions, medium chopped	1/2 cup	4. Mix well and season to taste.
Parsley, medium chopped	1/2 cup	5. If dressing is too dry, add some of the liquid in which giblets were cooked.
Garlic, medium chopped	2 cloves	
Oysters	1 qt.	
Giblets, cooked, medium chopped	from 1 bird	
Corn Bread, crumbled	3 cups	
Sage	1 tsp.	
Salt	to taste	
Black Pepper	to taste	
Cayenne Pepper	to taste	

BROCCOLI AND WILD RICE CASSEROLE

(This creamy dish is gourmet fare with any meat and beautiful with wild game)

YIELD: 12 PORTIONS   24 PORTIONS

INGREDIENTS	12 PORTIONS	24 PORTIONS	METHOD
Broccoli, cooked, chopped	2-1/2 lb.	5 lb.	Combine ingredients, place in buttered pan, and bake in oven at 400°F. for 30 minutes.
Wild Rice, cooked	1-1/2 lb.	3 lb.	
Onion, Medium-Sized, chopped	1/2	1	
Cream of Celery Soup	2 cans (10-1/2 oz.)	1 can (46 oz.)	
Milk	1 cup	2 cups	
Cream Cheese	1-1/2 pkg. (12 oz.)	3 pkg. (12 oz.)	
Salt	to taste	to taste	
Pepper	to taste	to taste	
Flavor Enhancer	to taste	to taste	

LOUISIANA RED BEANS

(These well-seasoned, creamy beans were standard fare once a week in the South)

YIELD:	5 PORTIONS	20 PORTIONS
INGREDIENTS		
Red Beans *or* Kidney Beans	1/2 lb.	2 lb.
Smoked Sausage, sliced	1/2 lb.	2 lb.
Onion, medium dice	1/2	2
Garlic, chopped	1/2 clove	2 cloves
Ham Bone	1	1
Bay Leaf	1	2
Cayenne Pepper	dash	dash
Cumin	to taste	to taste
Salt	to taste	to taste
Pepper	to taste	to taste

METHOD

1. Wash and pick over beans; cover with cold water and soak overnight.
2. Cook sausage, onion, and garlic until slightly brown.
3. Add beans and water in which they have been soaking, ham bone, and more water to cover.
4. Add seasonings and simmer, covered, several hours until beans become creamy.
5. Correct the seasonings and serve with rice and cornbread.

ALMOND CRESCENTS

(Chopped pecans and almond paste flavor delicate cookies)

YIELD:	45 COOKIES	90 COOKIES
INGREDIENTS		
Almond Paste	7/8 cup	14 oz.
Confectioners' Sugar	3/4 cup	12 oz.
Almond Flavoring	1/2 tsp.	1 tsp.
Pecans, chopped	1 cup	8 oz.
Egg Whites, beaten	as needed	as needed

METHOD

1. Combine almond paste with sugar and almond flavoring; when well combined, stir in pecans.
2. Add egg whites as needed to make a firm dough that is easily handled, being careful that it is not too soft.
3. Shape into crescents on greased baking sheets and bake in oven at 350°F. until barely browned. Cool.

RUM MANGOES ★

(A recipe from Trinidad)

YIELD: 2 PORTIONS   20 PORTIONS

INGREDIENTS

Mangoes, Large,* Ripe, Firm	2	20
Rum	3 tbsp.	15 oz.
Bitters	2 dashes	2 tsp.

*If mangoes are small you will need 2 per person.

METHOD

1. Peel mangoes, cut meat into 1-inch cubes, discarding pits.
2. Combine rum and bitters in a bowl; carefully mix in mango cubes.
3. Cover and chill.
4. Serve as is or top with sugar and whipped cream.

New Orleans Country Club

★ See recipe, facing page.

RUM MANGOES

Angostura
Aromatic
Bitters

Oahu Country Club

Honolulu, Hawaii

History has it that the original Hawaiians were a happy people who loved to eat, drink, and be merry. Islanders today fit the same mold, whatever their origins, and the Oahu Country Club carries on the old customs on 300 acres once owned by King Kamehameha III.

The tract in Waolani Valley, covered with guava bushes and Hilo grass, had been in the hands of the English Rooke family for more than 70 years when the club acquired it in 1906. A stream ran through the grounds, and the clubhouse site afforded a magnificent view from the pali across the whole sweep of Nuuanu Valley to the harbor. Today, from the same site, one looks down the valley to bustling Honolulu.

The club's cuisine reflects the multi-racial background of Hawaii. The sandwich list features Teriyaki Steak Sandwich Osaka, Kona Coast Mahimahi (fillet of the delicate fish served with tartar sauce), and Prawns Polynesian (bananas, celery, and prawns or shrimp served open-faced on a bun), as well as mainland favorites.

Oahu Country Club is famous for its pineapple-spiked iced tea which is a cross between iced mint tea and fruit punch. It is made by steeping mint leaves with the tea for 3 minutes. For a 14-in. glass, the mint tea is combined with 1 tbsp. of pineapple juice and 1 tbsp. of sugar.

YOKOHAMA SOUP

(Spinach, celery, clam juice, fish stock, and sauterne combine flavors in this favorite from the South Seas)

YIELD:	6 PORTIONS	24 PORTIONS
INGREDIENTS		
Celery, thinly sliced	1 rib	4 ribs
Onion, thinly sliced	1	4
Butter	2 tbsp.	1/2 cup
Parsley, chopped	1 sprig	4 sprigs
Bay Leaves	2	8
Garlic, minced	1/2 tsp.	2 tsp.
Thyme	1/4 tsp.	1 tsp.
Sauterne	1 cup	4 cups
Flour	1 tbsp.	1/4 cup
Fish Stock	4 cups	4 gal.
Clam Juice	2 cups	2 qt.
Salt	to taste	to taste
White Pepper	to taste	to taste
Flavor Enhancer	to taste	to taste
Worcestershire Sauce	to taste	to taste
Spinach, chopped	1/4 cup	1 cup
Half-and-Half, heated	1 cup	4 cups
Heavy Cream, whipped	1 cup	4 cups

METHOD

1. Quickly saute celery and onion in butter but do not brown.
2. Add parsley, bay leaves, garlic, and thyme.
3. Pour in wine and simmer until reduced to one-half.
4. Combine flour with some of the above mixture; stir into remaining reduced mixture.
5. Add fish stock and clam juice; bring to a boil and simmer.
6. Season with salt, white pepper, flavor enhancer and Worcestershire sauce.
7. Strain; add cooked spinach and heated cream.
8. Top each serving with a dollop of unsweetened whipped cream; glaze under a salamander or broiler.

HOT KING CRAB SALAD

(Mushroom slices and shreds of cabbage join crabmeat in a tangy dressing. The entree is served hot in individual portions)

YIELD:	2 PORTIONS	24 PORTIONS
INGREDIENTS		
Crabmeat, cut in 1/2-inch dice	8 oz.	6 lb.
Cabbage, thinly shredded	4 oz.	3 lb.
Mushrooms, sliced	4 oz.	3 lb.
Chives, chopped	2 tbsp.	1-1/2 cups
Onion, minced	2 tbsp.	1-1/2 cups
Prepared Mustard	1 tbsp.	3/4 cup
Mayonnaise	about 3/4 cups	about 9 cups
Salt	1 tsp.	4 tbsp.
White Pepper	few grains	2 tsp.
Worcestershire Sauce	1 dash	1 tbsp.
Lemon Juice	1/2 tsp.	2 tbsp.

METHOD

1. Mix first 5 ingredients in a stainless steel bowl.
2. Combine mustard with enough mayonnaise to bind ingredients; add salt, ground white pepper, a dash of Worcestershire sauce, and lemon juice to taste.
3. Stir dressing into crab mixture; mound into individual baking shells. Cover 1/4 inch thick with mayonnaise. Bake in oven at 450°F. for 10 to 15 minutes.

Oahu Country Club

Offutt Officers' Club

Offutt Air Force Base, Nebraska

The Offutt Air Force Base is the home of the Strategic Air Command, and it is located on the Nebraska prairie, near Omaha. This is where the buttons will be pushed to send the ballistic missiles out of their silos all across the continent, should the word come that the country has been attacked.

The club is a popular spot for rest and relaxation. Special parties are an everyday occurrence at the club, where SAC officers entertain distinguished civilian, government, and military personnel who have come to confer with them from all over the world.

The favorite cocktail party fare for the predominantly masculine affairs is a steamship round of beef, buns, mustard and catsup, horseradish and mayonnaise, with perhaps a few pickles, a dip or two, and whatever else the host may fancy. What most of the men fancy is the beef.

Food at the club is mostly midwestern fare designed to stick to the ribs and keep the men warm when the winter winds blow. It is good country cooking done with great pride by good local cooks.

CHILLED CUCUMBER SOUP

(Dill flavors this cool summer favorite)

YIELD:	8 PORTIONS	24 PORTIONS
INGREDIENTS		
Cucumbers	6	18
Onion	1/4	3/4
Buttermilk	1 qt.	3 qt.
Sour Cream	1 pt.	3 pt.
Dill	1 tsp.	1 tbsp.
Salt	to taste	to taste
Pepper	to taste	to taste

Note   This needs considerable salt.

METHOD

1. Peel cucumbers and cut lengthwise, saving enough to slice thinly for garnish. Remove as many seeds as possible. Grind in blender with onion.
2. Blend buttermilk and sour cream; add cucumber, onion, and dill.
3. Season to taste and chill.
4. Garnish with cucumber slices.

BEEF TENDERLOIN TIPS AND NOODLES

(Individual casseroles of noodles topped with tender beef and gravy)

YIELD:	6 to 8 PORTIONS	24 PORTIONS
INGREDIENTS		
Beef Tenderloin	3 lb.	10 lb.
Beef Broth	1 qt.	3 qt.
Worcestershire Sauce	1 tsp.	1 tbsp.
Bottled Browning Sauce	1 tsp.	1 tbsp.
Cornstarch	4 tsp.	1/4 cup
Noodles *or* Rice	as needed	as needed

METHOD

1. Broil beef tenderloin until medium rare; cut in bite-sized chunks.
2. Blend together the beef broth, Worcestershire sauce, and bottled browning sauce; bring to a boil.
3. Blend some water with cornstarch and add the smooth mixture to the broth, whipping constantly until thickened and smooth.
4. Add meat and bring again to serving temperature.
5. Stir some of the sauce through hot, buttered noodles or rice and serve in individual casseroles, spooning meat in sauce over noodles or rice.

WESTERN NEBRASKA BEER BEANS

(Canned beans gone glamorous for the barbecue)

YIELD:	10 PORTIONS	100 PORTIONS	METHOD
INGREDIENTS			1. Chop onion and fry in butter.
Onion, chopped	1/4 cup	1 lb.	2. Add catsup, mustard, and canned Pork And
Butter	1-1/2 tbsp.	1/4 lb.	Beans.
Catsup	3 tbsp.	16 oz.	3. Add brown sugar to beer and mix into beans.
Mustard	1-1/2 tbsp.	8 oz.	4. Lay bacon on top.
Pork And Beans	2/3 can	6 cans	5. Bake in oven at 275°F. for 1 hour.
	(10 oz.)	(10 oz.)	
Brown Sugar	2 tsp.	3 oz.	
Beer	1/2 cup	1 qt.	
Bacon Slices	1	6	

HOT GERMAN POTATO SALAD, NEBRASKA STYLE

(Actually improves in flavor as it stands)

YIELD:	5 PORTIONS	50 PORTIONS	METHOD
INGREDIENTS			1. Cook unpeeled potatoes and peel while hot; slice or dice.
Potatoes	1 lb.	10 lb.	2. Combine potatoes, celery, onion, and parsley.
Celery, thinly sliced	1 rib	1 lb.	3. Fry bacon; crumble and add with the bacon fat to hot water, vinegar, salt, and pepper.
Onion, medium dice	1/4 cup	1 lb.	4. Pour this dressing over potato mixture; combine gently; cover and let stand for 30 to 40 minutes to season well. Serve hot.
Parsley, finely chopped	1 tsp.	1 oz.	
Bacon	3 slices	1-1/2 lb.	
Water	1/3 cup	3-3/4 cups	
Vinegar	1-1/2 tbsp.	1 cup	
Salt	1-1/2 tsp.	1/3 cup	
Pepper	pinch	1 tsp.	

The Omaha Club

Omaha, Nebraska

Nebraska seems like a "new" state, but the Omaha Club's original club-house dated back to 1895. The club's present four-story structure was erected on the downtown site of the original club and incorporates many of the original fireplaces, a gracious circular stairway, the chandeliers, and Jacobean furniture from the old club.

The men's bar is identified by an old motto outside the door which reads: "Where women cease to trouble and the wicked are at rest."

True to one of their major industries, the Nebraskans demand that a standing rib of beef be featured on every menu, appear on every buffet, and be incorporated into every special party.

The Omaha Club

DOVER SOLE MEUNIERE

(Not a fillet, but a whole sole beautifully flavored and served with Sauce Meuniere)

YIELD: 1 PORTION   20 PORTIONS

INGREDIENTS		
Dover Sole, Whole, skinned, with head and fins removed	1 lb.	20 lb.
Salt	to taste	to taste
Lemon, juice of	1/2	10
Worcestershire Sauce	3 dashes	4 tsp.
Flour	1 tbsp.	1 cup
Oil	1 tbsp.	1 cup
Butter	1 tsp.	1/2 cup
Fresh Parsley, chopped	1 tsp.	2 tbsp.

METHOD

1. Brush skinned sole with salt, lemon juice, and Worcestershire sauce.
2. Flour sole and saute to a golden brown in oil.
3. To make the Sauce Meuniere, drain oil from pan and add butter. Melt butter until lightly browned and add a few drops of lemon juice and Worcestershire sauce. Sprinkle with parsley.
4. Cover sole with Sauce Meuniere and serve.

ROAST RACK OF VENISON DIANE

(Venison roasted with white wine and served with a rich sauce flavored with currant jelly)

YIELD: 2 PORTIONS

INGREDIENTS	
Rack of Venison	1 24-ounce rack
Salt	to taste
Pepper	to taste
Carrot, chopped	1/2
Onion, chopped	1/2
Celery, chopped	1 rib
Bay Leaf	1
Whole Clove	1
Rosemary	1/4 tsp.
Paprika	1/4 tsp.
White Wine	1 cup
Brown Gravy Mix	1 small pkg.
Water	1/2 cup
Heavy Cream	1/2 cup
Currant Jelly	1 tsp.

METHOD

1. Season the venison with salt and pepper. Roast in oven at 450° for five minutes.
2. Add carrot, onion, celery, bay leaf, clove, rosemary, paprika, and white wine; roast 15 minutes longer.
3. Remove the venison.
4. To the liquid in the pan, add the gravy mix and the water. Stir well, heat, and strain.
5. Add heavy cream and currant jelly to strained mixture. Serve sauce over carved rack.

Petroleum Club, Houston

Houston, Texas

The Petroleum Club, capping Houston's 44-story Exxon building, derives all of its design elements in some way from oil. That sounds a bit murky, but it is done with such imagination, good taste, and attention to unifying detail that the result is quietly impressive in a very modern way.

The room which serves as both a ballroom and main dining room is dominated by a tapestry depicting a cross-section of the earth's strata from a point on the Gulf Coast near Houston to the Permian Basin of West Texas. The designer consulted with members of the club who are geologists and translated their story to eight looms. The actual weaving, done in Spain, uses 287 specially dyed yarns in the earth colors—black, grey, and rusty orange—which are repeated throughout the club. Similar care was taken with all of the club's furnishings and decor.

The menu is international in scope, but each day's luncheon menu features, as one of 3 Chef's Suggestions, an "East Texas Country Dinner." Here appear such favorites as fried smoked country bacon with collard greens and pinto beans. They use to call this country food suggestion the "Dry Hole Special." Recently one of the members commented there had been too many dry holes lately, so the name has been changed, but the variety of East Texas fare flows on.

SNAPPER BEURRE BLANC

(Poached red snapper with a rich wine-butter sauce)

YIELD:	6 PORTIONS	24 PORTIONS
INGREDIENTS		
Red Snapper Fillets, 6 Ounce	6	24
Dry White Wine	1/2 cup	2 cups
Fish Stock (recipe, p. 235)	1 cup	1 qt.
Shallots, chopped	1/4 cup	1 cup
Sweet Butter	1/2 cup	1 lb.
Salt	to taste	to taste
White Pepper	to taste	to taste
Lemon Juice	to taste	to taste

METHOD

1. Poach red snapper fillets in a broth made of white wine and fish stock.
2. Remove fillets; add shallots; simmer to reduce volume to 1/5. Remove pan from heat and slowly add butter, bit by bit, moving the pan constantly in a circular motion. Do not overheat or the butter will break down.
3. Season with salt, pepper, and lemon juice. The sauce will be light and creamy. Pour over warm fillets and serve.

LANGOUSTINES A LA MODE

(Large Spanish shrimp stuffed with lobster, then poached in wine and fish stock—the dish is finished off in the broiler and served with a trifle of truffle)

YIELD:	3 PORTIONS	24 PORTIONS
INGREDIENTS		
Royal Spanish Shrimp	6	48
Brazilian Lobster Meat,	8 oz.	4 lb.
Heavy Cream, whipped	1/3 cup	16 oz.
Egg White, beaten	1/2	4
Brandy	1 dash	1-1/2 tbsp.
Salt	as needed	as needed
Pepper	as needed	as needed
Flavor Enhancer	as needed	as needed
Dry White Wine	as needed	as needed
Fish Stock (recipe, p. 235)	as needed	as needed
Beurre Manie (recipe, p. 234)	as needed	as needed
Hollandaise Sauce (recipe, p. 226)	as needed	as needed
Heavy Cream, whipped	as needed	as needed
Truffle, sliced	as needed	as needed

METHOD

1. Shell raw shrimp, leaving tail fin on; make a lengthwise incision.
2. Fold lobster meat into combined whipped cream, egg white, brandy, salt, pepper, and flavor enhancer; use to fill the shrimp.
3. In the oven, poach the shrimp until warmed through in a broth made with 1/3 wine to 2/3 fish stock. Reduce broth by half and bind with Beurre Manie.
4. Combine a little Hollandaise and whipped cream. Pour over the shrimp and glaze in the broiler.
5. Garnish with truffle.

CRABMEAT IMPERIAL
(Easy and elegant)

YIELD:	5 PORTIONS	20 to 24 PORTIONS	
INGREDIENTS			**METHOD**
Butter	3 tbsp.	6 oz. (12 tbsp.)	Saute in butter the onion, green pepper, mushrooms, and pimiento. Add crabmeat, fish sauce, and heavy cream. Bring to a boil and spoon into oval dishes for portion servings. Sprinkle with Parmesan cheese and bake in a hot oven until mixture bubbles.
Onion, chopped	1/2 cup	2 cups	
Green Pepper, diced	1/2 cup	2 cups	
Mushrooms, diced	1/2 cup	2 cups	
Pimiento, diced	1/2 cup	2 cups	
Lump Crabmeat	1 lb.	4 lb.	
Fish Sauce*	2 cups	2 qt.	
Heavy Cream	1 cup	1 qt.	
Parmesan Cheese	as needed	as needed	

*Fish sauce is fish stock thickened with a roux to a medium consistency (recipes, pp. 233, 235).

RATATOUILLE NICOISE
(Marvelous with omelets and crepes; delicious as a vegetable side dish)

YIELD:	5 to 6 PORTIONS	24 PORTIONS	
INGREDIENTS			**METHOD**
Green Pepper	1	4	1. Dice green pepper, eggplant, squash, onion, and tomatoes into 1-inch squares; saute in olive oil.
Eggplant, Medium-Sized	1	4	2. Add tomato paste, garlic, and seasonings.
Zucchini Squash, Medium-Sized	1	4	3. Braise in oven at 325°F. for approximately 1/2 to 3/4 hour.
Onion	1/2	2	
Tomatoes	2	8	
Olive Oil	as needed	as needed	
Tomato Paste	2 tbsp.	4 oz. (1/2 cup)	
Garlic, pressed	1 clove	4 cloves	
Salt	to taste	to taste	
Pepper	to taste	to taste	
Thyme	to taste	to taste	

THE FLAMING DERRICK
(Shrimp and beef flambeed on a skewer)

YIELD:	6 PORTIONS	24 PORTIONS
INGREDIENTS		
Tenderloin Tips, 1-inch cubes	1 lb.	4 lb.
Olive Oil	1/2 cup	2 cups
Garlic, mashed	1 clove	4 cloves
Thyme	1/2 tsp.	2 tsp.
Oregano	1/2 tsp.	2 tsp.
Black Pepper	1/2 tsp.	2 tsp.
Shrimp, Raw, peeled	12	48
Cherry Tomatoes	12	48
Green Pepper, 2-inch squares	6 sqs.	24 sqs.
Fresh Mushrooms, Whole	24	96
Onions, Small, Whole	12	48
Salt	to taste	to taste
Pepper	to taste	to taste
White Rice, cooked	6 cups	24 cups
Bamboo Shoots	2 cups	8 cups
Red Wine	1 cup	1 qt.
Brandy	2 tbsp.	1/2 cup

METHOD

1. Marinate tenderloin tips in olive oil, garlic, thyme, oregano, and pepper for 24 hours.
2. Alternate marinated meat on a skewer with raw shrimp, cherry tomatoes, green pepper squares, mushrooms, and onions. Season with salt and pepper. Pre-broil in the kitchen.
3. Finish broiling at the table, if desired. Serve on a bed of rice and bamboo shoots with a sauce made from red wine and flaming brandy.

Petroleum Club, Houston

Pinehurst Country Club

Littleton, Colorado

Here is a club that planned its clubhouse around the club menu, because of the belief that the heart of a good club is good food. The clientele was considered, the menus were planned, the kitchen was designed, and then the building planners moved on to the rest of the clubhouse.

The site of this award-winning kitchen (surrounded by the lovely clubhouse and 18 holes of golf) is a suburb of Denver. For 1 week each July the club's manager offers incantations to the gods who hide in the nearby Rocky Mountains . . . praying that the gods will keep a tight rein on the rain. Sunshine is a necessary ingredient for the club's week-long Hawaiian Holiday. Naturally, rain means trouble. The week's schedule includes:

On successive Saturday nights, two identical full-scale luaus
On the Sunday between, a golfers' event with a Hawaiian buffet
On Tuesday, a "pee wee luau" for 6- to 12-year olds
On Wednesday, a teen luau for 13- to 19-year olds
On Thursday, an Aloha fashion show luncheon featuring Hawaiian fashions flown to the mainland and sold by a local dress shop.

So popular is all of this South Pacific activity and food that the club still has problems. Two Saturday luaus no longer accommodate all of the members who would like to come and enjoy, in the shadow of the Rockies, suckling pig, Hukilau Celestial Chicken, Curried Shrimp and Cabbage in Coconut Milk, Tropical Chicken Fruit Salad Mold, and other such Polynesian delights.

CURRIED SHRIMP AND CABBAGE IN COCONUT MILK

(A Polynesian dish that is particularly popular for luaus)

YIELD:	10 PORTIONS	600 PORTIONS	METHOD
INGREDIENTS			1. Saute the shrimp in olive oil.
Shrimp	1-1/4 lb.	75 lb.	2. Sprinkle with curry powder and paprika.
Olive Oil	1/4 cup	1 gal.	3. Stir in cabbage and leek.
Curry Powder	1/4 tsp.	4 tbsp.	4. Heat the milk and shredded coconut to-
Paprika	1/8 tsp.	2 tsp.	gether for 2 hours.
Cabbage, cut in			5. Just before serving, combine coconut milk
2-inch dice	1/4 head	10 lb.	with other ingredients.
Leek, cut in			
2-inch dice	1	10 lb.	
Milk	1/2 cup	2 gal.	
Coconut, shredded	1/4 cup	3 lb.	

Pinehurst Country Club

TROPICAL CHICKEN FRUIT SALAD MOLD
(A favorite at luaus, buffets, and summer luncheons)

YIELD:	8 PORTIONS	24 PORTIONS
INGREDIENTS		
Gelatin,		
Lemon Flavor	1 tbsp.	3 tbsp.
Water, boiling	2 cups	6 cups
Chicken, cooked, diced	1 cup	3 cups
Pineapple, crushed,		
drained	1 cup	3 cups
Papaya, diced	1/2	1-1/2
Mango, diced larger		
than chicken	1	3
Cottage Cheese, Large		
Curd, Cream-style	1/2 cup	1-1/2 cups

METHOD
1. Dissolve gelatin in water and chill until syrupy.
2. Combine remaining ingredients, stir into gelatin, and pour into molds. Chill until firm.

POLYNESIAN RICE
(A quick, hot pudding with pineapple and raisins)

YIELD:	10 PORTIONS	50 PORTIONS
INGREDIENTS		
Rice, cooked	1 lb.	5 lb.
Coconut, shredded	1/4 cup	1/2 lb.
Raisins	1/4 cup	1/2 lb.
Crushed Pineapple,		
drained	1 cup	2 lb.

METHOD
Combine all ingredients and serve hot.

Pinnacle Club

New York, New York

One of the loftiest clubs in New York City is the Pinnacle, located atop the Mobile Building on Manhattan Island. From the wining and dining areas, members have a spectacular view of all of Manhattan, the neighboring boroughs, and the spans that bring the workers in to labor for their daily bread.

The Pinnacle is famed for its daily bread, cake, and pastries—all made on the premises. Each morning the pastry chef even bakes fresh croissants and muffins, which a waiter with a bun warmer offers to members in the dining room, together with hard rolls and thinly sliced black bread that has been brushed with melted butter, sprinkled liberally with Parmesan cheese, and broiled. This crisp pumpernickel is so popular that members often carry it home to reheat at cocktail time.

One of the features of the club menu is an item called "Today's International," identified by the United Nations emblem (the U. N. building looms large in the view to the east from the dining room). A short description of the featured ethnic dish assists members in ordering. The foreign specialty changes each day, and the ethnic cuisine from which the next day's entree will be chosen is identified to lure lovers of a special kind of food back the following day.

MONA LISA DRESSING

(A sharp, creamy dressing for salads, fish, beef, or ham)

YIELD:	2 CUPS	12 CUPS
INGREDIENTS		
Mayonnaise	1 cup	6 cups
Horseradish	1 tbsp.	1/3 cup
Paprika	1/2 tbsp.	3 tbsp.
English Mustard	1/2 tbsp.	3 tbsp.
Sour Cream	1/2 cup	3 cups
Chives, chopped	1/2 tbsp.	3 tbsp.
Chili Sauce	2 tbsp.	3/4 cup

METHOD

Combine all ingredients. Allow flavors to combine a few hours before use.

BAKED LAMB OR MUTTON CHOPS CHAMP VALLON ★

(Men love these chops and potatoes baked together with onion and garlic)

YIELD:	6 PORTIONS	24 PORTIONS
INGREDIENTS		
Lamb *or* Mutton Chops, Thick	6	24
Potatoes, sliced	4 lb.	16 lb.
Onion, sliced	10 oz.	40 oz.
Butter	2 oz.	1/2 lb.
Garlic, minced	1 clove	4 cloves
Salt	1 tbsp.	1/4 cup
Pepper	1/2 tbsp.	2 tbsp.
Water *or* Stock	1 qt.	1 gal.

METHOD

1. Season and brown the lamb chops on both sides.
2. Place chops in large baking dish with remaining ingredients.
3. Bake uncovered in oven at 350°F. for about 1-1/2 hours.

★ See picture, facing page.

BAKED LAMB OR MUTTON CHOPS CHAMP VALLON

The
American
Lamb Council

SAUCE GRIBICHE

(Herbs, pickles, onion, and egg make this an exciting, light sauce for meat or fish)

YIELD:	6 PORTIONS	24 PORTIONS
INGREDIENTS		
French Dressing	1 cup	4 cups
Sour Pickles, finely chopped	2	8
Fresh Tarragon, finely chopped	1 tbsp.	1/4 cup
Chervil, finely chopped	1 tbsp.	1/4 cup
Parsley, finely chopped	1 tbsp.	1/4 cup
Chives, finely chopped	1 tbsp.	1/4 cup
Onion, finely chopped	1 tbsp.	1/4 cup
Egg, hard-cooked	1	4

METHOD

Combine all ingredients and serve as a sauce over meat or fish.

Quinnipiack Club

New Haven, Connecticut

"To a foreigner, a Yankee is an American. To an American, a Yankee is a Northerner. To a Northerner, a Yankee is a New Englander. To a New Englander, a Yankee is a Vermonter. To a Vermonter, a Yankee is one who eats pie for breakfast."

E. F. Phillips, director of Stanford Museum in Nature Center, Connecticut, is credited with having said it first, and by his definition the Quinnipiack Club, New Haven, Connecticut, has a host of Yankees as members. A small steak and a big slice of fresh, hot pie make a favorite breakfast for early risers at the club.

Another regional favorite, the New England boiled dinner, is not considered truly "New England" unless made with "bully beef" (fresh brisket). The beef is "nipped up" with horseradish sauce to keep the taste buds in trim.

The club's secret for preparing Long Island duckling is to roast the birds over a 2-day period so that they are completely rendered of fat and there is no possibility of any slightly fishy flavor. After the first roasting, the duck is boned. The second day, when the duck is finished off for serving, it looks like a portion of half duckling, easily cut and eaten. Wild duck can be prepared the same way.

An old-fashioned shore dinner is another traditional New England meal. Here the meal begins with clam fritters and clam chowder, then moves on to steamed clams. When the clams have given their all, fresh fish (halibut or swordfish) and french fries take over. Then comes lobster, either broiled or boiled, served with steamy, golden sweet corn. Indian Pudding, Bread Pudding, or Rice Pudding cap the Connecticut menu.

CHESTNUT STUFFING

(A New World twist to an Old World favorite)

YIELD:	15 CUPS	60 CUPS
INGREDIENTS		
Chestnuts	2-1/2 lb.	10 lb.
Onion, chopped	1-1/2 cups	6 cups
Celery, chopped	1-1/2 cups	6 cups
Butter	1/2 lb.	2 lbs.
Bread Crumbs, dry	6 cups	1-1/2 gal.
Salt	1-1/2 tsp.	2 tbsp.
Thyme	3/4 tsp.	1 tbsp.
Marjoram	3/4 tsp.	1 tbsp.
Sage	3/4 tsp.	1 tbsp.

METHOD

1. Crack shells of chestnuts and simmer 5 minutes. While hot, remove shells and skins. Boil shelled nuts approximately 30 minutes, or until tender; chop fine.
2. Saute onion and celery in butter until lightly browned. Mix with crumbs, seasonings, and prepared chestnuts.

FRENCH APPLE PIE ★

(Have your pie and icing, too)

YIELD:	1 PIE	4 PIES
INGREDIENTS		
Apples, peeled, sliced	7	28
Pastry for Double-Crust Pie(s)		
Sugar	1 cup	4 cups
Flour	1/4 cup	1 cup
Cinnamon	1 tsp.	4 tsp.
Nutmeg	1 tsp.	4 tsp.
Lemon Juice	2 tsp.	4 tsp.
Butter	1/2 cup	2 cups
Raisins, plumped*		

METHOD

1. Arrange apple slices in unbaked pie shell.
2. Combine remaining ingredients and pour over apple slices.
3. Cover with remaining pastry and bake in preheated oven at 425°F. for 20 minutes.
4. Lower temperature to 350°F. and bake 40 minutes longer.
5. Cool and frost with Confectioners' Glaze.**

*To plump raisins, soak in water to cover overnight, or bring to simmering temperature and cool.
**Glaze is made by stirring together confectioners' sugar and water, milk, wine, or fruit juice to a thin consistency.

★ See picture, facing page.

FRENCH APPLE PIE

The
Apple
Institute

QUINNIPIACK PLUM PUDDING

(An old-fashioned steamed pudding stuffed with spices, fruits, and peels)

YIELD:	1 QUART MOLD	1 to 2 QUART MOLD
INGREDIENTS		
Flour	1/4 cup plus 2 tbsp.	3/4 cup
Salt	1/2 tsp.	1 tsp.
Baking Soda	1/2 tsp.	3/4 tsp.
Cinnamon	1/2 tsp.	1 tsp.
Mace	1/4 tsp.	1/2 tsp.
Nutmeg	1/8 tsp.	1/4 tsp.
Raisins, chopped	1/2 cup	1/2 lb.
Currants	1/2 cup	1/2 lb.
Candied Mixed Fruits	1/4 cup	1/2 cup
Candied Orange Peel	1/4 cup	1/2 cup
Candied Lemon Peel	1/4 cup	1/2 cup
Zwieback Crumbs, fine	1/4 cup	1/2 cup
Milk, hot	1/4 cup plus 2 tbsp.	3/4 cup
Brown Sugar	1/2 cup	1 cup
Eggs, separated	3 small	5 large
Suet, finely chopped	1 cup	1 lb.
Orange Juice	2 tbsp.	1/4 cup
Strawberry Jelly	1/3 cup	6 oz.

METHOD

1. Sift together flour, salt, soda, and spices; mix in fruits and peels.
2. Soften crumbs in hot milk for 5 minutes.
3. Beat brown sugar into egg yolks; add suet and crumbs; stir into flour/fruit mixture. Add juice and jelly.
4. Fold in beaten egg whites.
5. Pour into well-greased and floured mold; cover and steam for 3-1/2 hours.
6. Serve with Rich Brandy Sauce.

Quinnipiack Club

RICH BRANDY SAUCE
(A rich, fluffy sauce which holds well)

YIELD:	3 to 4 CUPS	7 to 8 CUPS	METHOD
INGREDIENTS			1. Gradually beat sugar into egg whites.
Granulated Sugar	1/2 cup	1 cup	2. Combine softened gelatine, whipped cream,
Egg Whites, beaten	3	6	and brandy; fold into egg whites.
Gelatine, Unflavored, dissolved in a little water	1/2 tsp.	1 tsp.	3. Chill until served.
Heavy Cream, whipped	1 cup	1 pt.	
Brandy	2-1/2 tbsp.	5 tbsp.	

QUINNIPIACK CLUB BREAD PUDDING
(Old-fashioned pudding that everybody loves)

YIELD:	6 PORTIONS	25 PORTIONS	METHOD
INGREDIENTS			1. Combine all ingredients and pour into greased baking dish. Bake in preheated oven at 350°F. for 1 hour.
Eggs, beaten	5	20	2. Serve with heavy cream or a Hot Buttered Rum Sauce, (recipe, p. 230).
Milk	1 qt.	1 gal.	
Sugar	1 cup	4 cups	
Bread, toasted, diced	6 slices	24 slices	
Salt	1/2 tsp.	2 tsp.	
Vanilla	1 tsp.	4 tsp.	
Raisins	1/2 cup	2 cups	

River Oaks Country Club

Houston, Texas

Visiting Houston in the summer, it is hard to believe that the River Oaks Country Club's 5 working fireplaces are ever used. One of them was moved south from an estate in New York.

But the fireplaces are used, and the 32-ft. long, polished table—acquired from a bank in Switzerland by way of an antique dealer in New Orleans—occasionally serves to hold some of the myriad dips and hors d'oeuvre featured at the big cocktail parties which are a popular way to entertain in Texas. They go on all evening with no dinner stop, but with ample supplies of hot and cold hors d'oeuvre and masses of finger foods served from beginning to end.

One of the River Oaks Country Club's cocktail party specials is a complete round of beef, weighing about 100 lb., with rump and shank still in place. The leg is roasted and then hung by a golden chain from a big wooden horse. Lights keep it hot the whole night long, and a chef slices and serves morsels on small, hot biscuits. They have been doing this for years at River Oaks, and it is still a good show.

A finger food recently added to the cocktail party list is oysters dipped in corn meal batter and deep fried. Tartar Sauce or a sour cream dill dip partners the oysters. There is always Mexican food with gallons of Chili con Queso disappearing each evening in the cocktail lounge. Another cocktail lounge favorite is peanut butter, spread on crackers. It goes well with highballs. Honest Injun!

CHILI CON QUESO

(Serve this hot cheese dip with fried tortilla chips, fritos, or corn chips)

YIELD: 1 GALLON

INGREDIENTS		METHOD
Hot Green Peppers, Small, diced	3	1. Saute peppers, onions, and garlic in bacon fat until onions are transparent; add tomatoes and seasonings; simmer 20 to 30 minutes.
Onions, Medium-Sized, diced	2	
Garlic, finely chopped	6 cloves	
Bacon Fat	as needed	
Tomatoes, chopped	1 qt.	2. Thicken with cornstarch which has been dissolved in water, then add grated cheese and stir while cheese melts.
Cumin Seed	1 tsp.	
Salt	to taste	
Pepper	to taste	
Cornstarch	1/4 cup	
Water	1 cup	
American Cheese, grated	3 lb.	

MEXICAN CAVIAR

(An inexpensive hors d'oeuvre)

YIELD:	25 2-TBSP. PORTIONS	100 2-TBSP. PORTIONS	METHOD
INGREDIENTS			1. Combine all ingredients.
Mexican Pink *or* Red Beans	3 cups	1 No. 10 can (12 cups)	2. When serving as an hors d'oeuvre, center "caviar" in a glass bowl surrounded with condiments of minced green chilis, chopped tomatoes, minced onions, chopped egg whites, and minced cucumber. Serve with tostadas and Melba toast rounds.
Green Onions, minced	1/4 cup	1 cup	
Green Pepper, minced	1/4 cup	1 cup	
Red Wine Vinegar	1/4 cup	1 cup	3. When using as a salad, serve on bed of romaine.
Olive Oil	1/2 cup	2 cups	
Salt	to taste	to taste	
Pepper	to taste	to taste	
Cumin	to taste	to taste	
Green Chilis (optional), minced			

CACAHUATE ★

(An unusual and very inexpensive Mexican cocktail dip that warms the tongue)

YIELD:	2 CUPS	10 CUPS
INGREDIENTS		
Green Fresadilla Tomatoes*	1/2 cup	2-1/4 cups
Chili Serrano**	1	6
Lard	1-1/2 tbsp.	1/2 cup
Peanut Butter	1-1/4 cups	6 cups
Cilantro (Coriander)***	to taste	to taste

METHOD

1. Peel and chop tomatoes and blend in liquidizer with chili.
2. Fry tomato-chili mixture in lard for about 5 minutes.
3. Remove from heat and cool well before adding peanut butter and cilantro.
4. Serve with tostadas.

*Green fresadilla tomatoes are a small tart variety that can be purchased in cans in Latin food stores.
**Chili Serrano is a bright green, smooth pepper, somewhat hot; available in cans.
***If Cilantro is not available in cans, dried coriander seed may be used.

RIVER OAKS POPPY SEED DRESSING

(Legend has it that Helen Corbitt was the first to use poppy seeds in her dressing for fruit salad)

YIELD:	1 PINT	10 GALLONS
INGREDIENTS		
Salad Oil	1-1/2 cups	6 gal.
Wine Vinegar	1/2 cup	2 gal.
White Corn Syrup*	5 tbsp.	5 qt.
Onion, finely grated	1/4	20
Dry Mustard	1/2 tbsp.	1-1/2 cups
Poppy Seeds	1 tbsp.	2 lb.

METHOD

1. Combine salad oil, vinegar, corn syrup, onion, and mustard until the oil disappears.
2. Add poppy seeds and mix a few minutes longer.
3. Store in wide-mouth plastic jars in refrigerator.

*To add to color and flavor, maraschino cherry juice can be used for a part of the syrup measure.

★ See picture, facing page.

CACAHUATE

Peanut
Associates,
Inc.

FRIED ASPARAGUS OR OKRA ★
(A crisp batter coats fresh lemon-flavored vegetables)

YIELD:	6 PORTIONS	24 PORTIONS
INGREDIENTS		
Fresh Asparagus *or* Fresh Okra	36 pieces	96 pieces
Lemon Juice	1 cup	1 qt.
Flour	1 cup	1 qt.
Salt	1 tsp.	4 tsp.
White Pepper	1/2 tsp.	2 tsp.
Eggs	2	8
Milk	1/4 cup	1 cup
Cracker Meal	2 cups	2 qt.
Peanut Oil	1 qt.	1 qt.

METHOD
1. Marinate vegetable in lemon juice for 1 to 2 hours; drain well.
2. Season flour with salt and pepper. Roll the vegetables in the mixture.
3. Make an egg-milk batter; dip floured vegetable into batter, then into cracker meal.
4. Fry in deep fat at 360°F. until a light, golden brown.
5. Serve as a finger hors d'oeuvre or as a vegetable.

BROCCOLI SOUFFLE
(Elegant luncheon fare and impressive—serve with Hollandaise Sauce)

YIELD:	5 PORTIONS	20 PORTIONS
INGREDIENTS		
Bacon, diced	1/4 lb.	1 lb.
Onion, diced	1/2 lb.	2 lb.
Broccoli, finely chopped	1-1/4 lb.	5 lb.
Heavy White Sauce (recipe, p. 237)	1/2 cup	2 cups
Egg Whites	3/4 cup	3 cups

METHOD
1. Saute bacon until crisp. Remove from pan. Pour off some of the grease in the pan.
2. Add onion to pan in which bacon was cooked and saute until tender.
3. Add bacon and onion to chopped broccoli, together with white sauce.
4. Whip egg whites to a stiff peak; fold into broccoli mixture.
5. Fill well-greased individual molds almost to the top. Place in a shallow baking pan with water about 1-inch deep. Cover with a wet towel.
6. Bake in oven at 350°F. for 20 to 25 minutes. Remove towel and put under broiler until surface is glazed.

★ See picture, facing page.

FRIED ASPARAGUS OR OKRA

Peanut
Associates,
Inc.

SOUTH OF THE BORDER CHICKEN

(Bake this tortilla-based favorite in individual casseroles or steam·table pans)

YIELD:	5 PORTIONS	30 PORTIONS
INGREDIENTS		
Chicken Breasts	5	30
Butter	3 tbsp.	8 oz. (1 cup)
Onion, Medium-Sized, chopped	1	6
Hot Green Pepper Sauce*	1 tsp.	2 tbsp.
Corn Tortillas	4	24
Milk	1-1/4 cups	7-1/2 cups
Cream of Mushroom Soup	1 can (10-1/2 oz.)	6 cans (10-1/2 oz.)
Cheddar Cheese, grated	1/2 cup	3/4 lb. (3 cups)

METHOD

1. Cut chicken breast into strips; saute in butter until lightly browned.
2. Add chopped onion and saute an additional 20 minutes. Add hot green pepper sauce (salsa).
3. Cut tortillas into 1-inch squares.
4. Place layers of chicken and layers of tortillas in greased baking pan.
5. Combine milk and mushroom soup; pour over chicken and top with cheese.
6. Bake in oven at 300°F. for 90 minutes.

*Hot green pepper sauce (salsa) can be purchased at any shop carrying Spanish or Mexican foods.

River Oaks Country Club

The Sanno

Tokyo, Japan

THE
SANNO

A specialty of this American Officers' Club in Japan is an Asian specialty called the Mongolian Barbecue. A special cooking plate is used—a large convex piece of iron, which looks a little like an automobile's hubcap or a disc from a harrow. The plate is about 3 ft. in diameter with rows of narrow grooves across the surface to carry fat and liquid off without their hitting the charcoal beneath.

Guests select the food they wish to have cooked, and the bowls go out to the man at the grill. He empties the bowl onto the cooking plate and within 4 minutes has vastly diminished the contents (leafy vegetables shrink tremendously). The cooked food goes back into the bowl and is served to the diner at his table.

The colorful selection of uncooked foods from which guests choose the raw materials for their Mongolian Barbecue includes thinly sliced beef, veal, pork, chicken, and turkey, each in its own labeled container. On top of the meats selected go the vegetables: a selection of shredded Chinese cabbage, strips of green pepper, small rings of green onion, celery chunks, wedges of leek, shredded chrysanthemum leaves, and chopped peanuts.

After guests have heaped their bowls with meats and vegetables, they ladle on "oils" for seasoning. The flavors are Japanese soy, garlic, ginger, hot spice, and caramel. Most of the "oils" are actually water flavored with the indicated ingredient. The exception is "Japanese soy" which is undiluted soy sauce.

TERIYAKI SWORDFISH
(The whole fish is marinated in a Chinese sauce before broiling)

INGREDIENTS

Swordfish	8 lb.
MARINADE	
Fish Stock, cold	3 cups
Soy Sauce	1/3 cup
Sugar	1 tbsp.
White Wine	1/2 cup
Ginger, Crushed	
or Powdered	2 tbsp.
Garlic Powder	dash

METHOD

1. Before broiling swordfish, marinate it for 30 minutes in sauce made by combining cold fish stock, soy sauce, sugar, wine, ginger, and garlic powder.
2. Drain fish well and broil over charcoal. Brush with sauce during cooking.

HONG KONG STEAK
(A ginger-sherry sauce tops thinly sliced beef on a bed of rice)

YIELD:

INGREDIENTS	12 PORTIONS	48 PORTIONS
Chicken Soup Base	1 tbsp.	1/4 cup
Cornstarch	1/3 cup	1-1/3 cups
Soy Sauce	1/3 cup	1-1/3 cups
Sugar	1 tbsp.	1/4 cup
Sherry	1/2 cup	2 cups
Ginger, Crushed		
or Powdered	1 tsp.	4 tsp.
Water *or* Stock	3 cups	3 qt.
Mushrooms, sliced	3/4 cup	3 cups
Sirloin *or* Flank		
Steak	3 lb.	12 lb.
Garlic	1/2 tsp.	2 tsp.

METHOD

1. Prepare sauce by combining the chicken soup base, cornstarch, soy sauce, sugar, sherry, ginger, and water or stock. Put in a saucepan and blend with a wire whip; heat until clear and thick. Add mushrooms.
2. Season sirloin steak with garlic and soy sauce. Broil.
3. Slice into thin slices and pour sauce over meat. Serve with rice.

PEKING PORK

(A delicious way to utilize cold pork roast)

YIELD:	6 PORTIONS	24 PORTIONS	
INGREDIENTS			METHOD
Pork Loin, cooked, sliced	18 ounces	4-1/2 lb.	1. Slice cold roast pork loin paper-thin.
Stock	3 cups	3 qt.	2. Broil, basting it with a teriyaki sauce made
Soy Sauce	1/3 cup	1-1/3 cups	by heating together stock, soy sauce, sugar,
Sugar	1 tbsp.	1/4 cup	white wine, ginger, and cornstarch.
White Wine	1/2 cup	2 cups	3. Saute the vegetables.
Crushed Ginger	1 tbsp.	1/4 cup	4. Serve vegetables on a plate topped with
Cornstarch	1/3 cup	1-1/3 cups	pork slices.
Celery, cut in 1-inch chunks	as needed	as needed	
Chinese Cabbage	as needed	as needed	
Snow Peas	as needed	as needed	
Bamboo Shoots	as needed	as needed	
Onion Rings	as needed	as needed	
Bean Sprouts	as needed	as needed	
Mushroom Slices	as needed	as needed	
Green Pepper Strips	as needed	as needed	

SUZIE WONG SANDWICH

(Ham, turkey, and cheese blend flavors in this rolled and fried favorite)

INGREDIENTS
Sandwich Loaf
Ham
Turkey Breast
American Cheese
Butter
Egg, beaten
Cooking Oil

METHOD

1. Slice uncut sandwich loaf into pieces 12-inches long and 1/2-inch thick. Each slice will make 2 sandwiches.
2. Place bread slice on either a wet napkin or waxed paper. Cover with 2 thin slices of ham, 1 thin slice of turkey breast, and 1 slice of American cheese.
3. Butter the bread. Roll sandwich and store in refrigerator. It will "settle" and become easy to cut. Cut sandwich roll in four pieces, dip in egg, and deep fry in oil to brown.

FRESH LEMON POLAR PIE

(A luscious dessert combining vanilla ice cream, lemon creme, and a fluffy meringue)

YIELD:	1 PIE	8 PIES
INGREDIENTS		
Butter	6 tbsp.	1-1/2 lb.
Sugar	7/8 cup	3-1/2 lb.
Salt	pinch	1 tsp.
Lemon Rind, grated	1 tbsp.	1/2 cup
Fresh Lemon Juice	1/3 cup	2-2/3 cups
Egg Yolks	3	24 (2 cups)
Egg	1	8
Ice Cream, Vanilla	1 pt.	4 qt.
Pastry Shell, baked	1	8
MERINGUE		
Egg Whites	3	24 (3 cups)
Cream of Tartar	1/4 tsp.	1-1/2 tsp.
Sugar	1/4 cup	1 lb.

METHOD

1. Melt butter; blend in sugar, salt, grated lemon rind, and fresh lemon juice.
2. Beat together the egg yolks and egg.
3. Stir some of hot lemon mixture into eggs. Add warm eggs to remaining lemon mixture and cook over simmering water, stirring frequently, until very thick and smooth. Cool.
4. Spread 1 pt. of softened ice cream into each pastry shell. Top each with 1 cup of the lemon mixture. Freeze.
5. Repeat layers, freezing after each addition.
6. To make Meringue, beat egg whites until frothy.
7. Add cream of tartar.
8. Gradually beat in sugar. Continue beating until mixture forms stiff peaks.
9. Spread pies with meringue, completely covering filling and sealing to edge of pastry.
10. Place on baking sheets filled with crushed ice. Brown in oven at 475°F. for 3 minutes.
11. Serve at once or freeze.

Somerset Club

Boston, Massachusetts

SOMERSET
CLUB

The Somerset Club is an old one, dating from 1846, and so is its home. One of the four adjacent houses facing Boston Common, which go to make the clubhouse, was designed by a famous Revolutionary War-period architect, A. Parris. The ornamental marble tablets on the front of the club were carved by Solomon Willard, the architect of the Bunker Hill Monument.

The staircase within one of these houses is an architect's and engineer's delight, spiralling up and around to serve 3 floors without a single supporting post.

Tradition is a sacred thing with this esteemed old club, and changes come slowly. Until 1968 the club was heated entirely by fireplaces, and there are working fireplaces in every room, each with a distinctly different mantel.

Each of the club's private dining rooms has its own Spode pattern, and there is a complete set of glassware in each butler's pantry. Butler-type service is used everywhere in the club, and no tray is ever taken into a dining room.

The club owns 21 pieces of Daniel Webster's silver. The Sheffield plate was brought to Philadelphia from Paris by Richard Rush, the American Minister to France, 1847 to 1849. He had purchased it from an old French family who had held it for 50 years. Upon purchase, Ambassador Rush had his own coat of arms engraved upon it. He and Daniel Webster were intimate friends and knowing that Webster admired the set, Rush offered to sell it. Some of Webster's admirers purchased it as a gift and had Webster's name engraved on the pieces. The silver is used once a year for a dinner honoring the club president.

BENGAL TOAST

(An unusual English Appetizer—ham and chutney with sour cream and Parmesan cheese)

YIELD:	16 PORTIONS	96 PORTIONS
INGREDIENTS		
Ham, boiled, finely diced	6 oz.	2-1/4 lb.
Sour Cream	1/4 cup	1-1/2 cups
White Bread	4 slices	24 slices
Chutney	as needed	as needed
Parmesan Cheese	as needed	as needed

METHOD

1. Combine boiled ham and sour cream.
2. Cut 16 rounds from 4 slices of white bread. Toast them and spread with ham mixture.
3. Dot each round with a good-sized piece of chutney. Sprinkle with Parmesan cheese.
4. Bake in oven at 400°F. for 3 minutes.

POTAGE CHOISEY

(A lovely lettuce soup to serve as an appetizer)

YIELD:	1-1/4 QUARTS	1 GALLON
INGREDIENTS		
Butter	3 tbsp.	6 oz. (12 tbsp.)
Leeks, minced	3	12
Onion, minced	1	4
Boston Lettuce, shredded	1/2 head	2 heads
Potatoes, sliced	2 cups	8 cups
Chicken Broth	3 cups	3 qt.
Cream	1 cup	4 cups
Salt	to taste	to taste
Pepper	to taste	to taste

METHOD

1. In a heavy saucepan, saute butter, leeks, and onion until mixture is transparent.
2. Add lettuce, potatoes, and chicken broth. Cover and cook slowly until potatoes are soft. Force through a food mill or puree in a blender.
3. Reheat at serving time in a double boiler, adding cream, salt, and pepper.

CLAM PIE

(Tender clams are cooked in wine, then baked in a creamy sauce under a pastry crust)

YIELD:	4 to 6 PORTIONS	24 PORTIONS
INGREDIENTS		
Clams	1 qt.	5 qt.
Dry White Wine	1 cup	5 cups
Peppercorns	3	15
Onion, Medium-Sized	1/2	3
Bay Leaf	1/2	3
Thyme	1/8 tsp.	1/2 tsp.
Butter	4 tbsp. (1/4 cup)	10 oz. (1-1/4 cups)
Flour	2 tbsp.	6 oz. (2/3 cup)
Milk	1/2 cup	2-1/2 cups
Cream	1/2 cup	2-1/2 cups
Salt	to taste	to taste
Pepper	to taste	to taste
Mushrooms, sliced	1/4 lb.	1-1/4 lb.
Sherry	3 tbsp.	1 cup
Salt	to taste	to taste
Pepper	to taste	to taste
Pastry	to cover 4 individual casseroles	to cover 24 individual casseroles

METHOD

1. Place in a kettle the clams, wine, peppercorns, onion, bay leaf, and thyme. Boil until clams open.
2. Strain the broth into a saucepan and allow clams to cool.
3. Make a cream sauce using clam broth for half the liquid, together with half of the butter and the flour, milk, cream, salt, and pepper.
4. Saute mushrooms in remaining butter.
5. Shuck the clams, removing black filament. Combine clams, mushrooms, and cream sauce. Add 3/4 of the sherry and the salt and pepper.
6. Put the mixture into deep pie dishes. Cover with pastry rolled quite thick. Make a hole in top and insert a small pastry tip, or little funnel, to permit steam to escape and to allow a little more sherry to be poured in before serving.

SQUABS EN CASSEROLE ★

(Madeira, mushrooms, and green Spanish olives enhance the squabs)

YIELD:	4 PORTIONS	24 PORTIONS
INGREDIENTS		
Squab	4	24
Butter	4 tbsp.	12 oz.
	(1/4 cup)	(1-1/2 cups)
Salt Pork, Lean, diced	1/2 lb.	3 lb.
Onions, Small, sliced	12	2 lb.
Mushrooms, sliced	1/4 lb.	1-1/2 lb.
Spanish Green Olives	12	72
Bay Leaf	1/2	3
Chicken Stock	1 cup	1-1/2 qt.
Madeira	1/4 cup	1-1/2 cups
Salt	to taste	to taste
Pepper	to taste	to taste

METHOD

1. Saute squabs in butter until well browned; transfer to a casserole.
2. Parboil salt pork for 3 minutes; add to butter in skillet, together with sliced onions and mushrooms. Saute until onions are pale yellow.
3. Add olives, bay leaf, chicken stock, wine, salt, and pepper. Bring to a boil and pour over squab in casserole. Bake in oven at 350°F. for 50 minutes.

TOMATOES SOMERSET

(An edible garniture—beautiful on a plate or surrounding a roast)

YIELD:	6 PORTIONS	24 PORTIONS
INGREDIENTS		
Tomatoes, Medium-Sized	6	24
Onion, minced	2 tsp.	3 tbsp.
White Bread Crumbs, soft	1 cup	1 qt.
Brown Sugar	1 tbsp.	1/4 cup
Butter, melted	2 tbsp.	1/2 cup
Salt	to taste	to taste
Pepper	to taste	to taste

METHOD

1. Remove the cores from the tomatoes; slice off tops and hollow out.
2. Combine the rest of the ingredients and stuff the tomatoes.
3. Place tomatoes in buttered baking dish and bake in oven at 350°F. for 15 to 20 minutes, or until top is browned.

★ See picture, facing page.

SQUABS EN CASSEROLE

Spanish
Green
Olive Commission

BEACON HILL OYSTERS

(Plump oysters in a celery sauce on toast)

YIELD:	4 PORTIONS	24 PORTIONS
INGREDIENTS		
Oysters	1 pt.	1-1/2 qt.
Celery, diced	2 cups	3 qt.
Water	1 cup	1-1/2 qt.
Butter	1/4 cup	1-1/2 cups
Flour	1/4 cup	1-1/2 cups
Cream	1 cup	6 cups
Salt	to taste	to taste
Pepper	to taste	to taste
Toast, buttered	as needed	as needed
Parsley, chopped	to garnish	to garnish

METHOD

1. Drain oysters, saving liquor.
2. Boil celery in salted water for 5 minutes. Remove the celery and boil water down to 3/4 cup. Make a roux by melting butter and stirring in flour. Cook 2 minutes over low heat.
3. Slowly add combined oyster and celery liquor; when smooth, add cream, salt, and pepper. Cook without boiling for 10 minutes.
4. Place oysters in moderately hot skillet. Cook until plump, removing the liquor and adding it to the sauce as it flows from the oysters.
5. Serve oysters on buttered toast, covered with the celery sauce and sprinkled with chopped parsley.

BAKED APPLES PARKMAN HAVEN

(Apples with spirit)

YIELD:	4 PORTIONS	24 PORTIONS
INGREDIENTS		
Apples, Large, cored	4	24
Brown Sugar	4 tbsp.	3/4 lb. (1-1/2 cups)
Cinnamon	1/2 tsp.	1 tbsp.
Cognac	4 tsp.	4 oz.

METHOD

1. Preheat oven to 400°F.
2. Place cored apples in a baking dish. Fill each cavity with 1 tbsp. brown sugar and 1/8 tsp. cinnamon.
3. Pour 1/8 inch water into the dish. Bake until apples are just tender but not collapsed (about 20 minutes), basting with syrup formed in baking dish. When apples are baked, add 1 tsp. cognac to each cavity.
4. Serve warm or cold with heavy cream.

Somerset Club

Statler Club

Ithaca, New York

The Statler Club is named to do homage to Ellsworth M. Statler, pioneer American hotelman, and the students enrolled in Cornell University's School of Hotel Administration participate in the operation of the club. The students need someone to practice on, and the faculty is only too willing to oblige. They are even willing to share. Guests of the University may use the club's main dining room, and seminar participants come under that heading.

The club does an excellent job of upholding Cornell's reputation as an innovator.

BLANCHARD RIDEOUT'S BEEF SOUP

(Red wine is the secret ingredient in this veg-beef melange)

YIELD:	2 QUARTS	5 GALLONS
INGREDIENTS		
Round Steak, cut in 1/2-inch cubes	2 lb.	20 lb.
Onions, diced	2	20
Water, boiling	2 qt.	5 gal.
Red Wine	1 cup	2-1/2 qt.
Carrots, peeled, sliced	4	40
Potatoes, Medium-Sized, peeled, cubed	3	30
Celery Ribs, sliced	3	30
Green Beans (optional)	as needed	as needed
Mushrooms (optional)	as needed	as needed
Salt	to taste	to taste
Bay Leaf	to taste	to taste
Thyme	to taste	to taste
Summer Savory	to taste	to taste
Parsley	to taste	to taste

METHOD

1. Brown cubed steak in vegetable oil.
2. Add onions; cover with half of the boiling water and all of the red wine.
3. Bring to a boil again, reduce heat, and cook gently an hour or more, until meat becomes tender.
4. Move to a large pot. Add remaining boiling water and vegetables; season to taste.
5. Simmer until done.

IMPERIAL CRAB

(Crab served in the shell with green pepper, pimiento, and mustard adding color and flavor)

YIELD:	6 PORTIONS	24 PORTIONS	METHOD
INGREDIENTS			
Backfin Crabmeat	1 lb.	4 lb.	1. Mix crabmeat with eggs and crumbs which have been moistened in milk.
Eggs	2	8	
Bread Crumbs	1/2 cup	2 cups	2. Add mustard, salt, pimiento, green pepper, cayenne, and butter; mix well.
Milk	1/2 cup	2 cups	
Mustard	dash	dash	3. Fill crab shells with mixture and dot with butter.
Salt	1 tsp.	4 tsp.	
Pimiento, diced	1/2 cup	2 cups	4. Brown quickly in hot oven at 500°F., being careful that filled shells do not burn.
Green Pepper, diced	1/2 cup	2 cups	
Cayenne Pepper	dash	dash	
Butter, melted	1/2 cup	2 cups	

COQ AU VIN

(Mushrooms and Burgundy wine make this chicken extra fine)

YIELD:	8 PORTIONS	24 PORTIONS	METHOD
INGREDIENTS			
Celery, diced	1/3 cup	1 cup	1. Saute celery, onion, and mushrooms until brown. Remove from fat. Save fat to fry chicken.
Onion, diced	1/3 cup	1 cup	
Mushrooms	1/3 cup	1 cup	
Chicken Fat *or* Butter	3 tbsp.	1/2 cup	2. Dredge chicken in flour. Saute in fat until brown.
Chicken	1	3	
Flour	2-1/2 tbsp.	1/2 cup	3. Remove chicken and thicken remaining fat with flour. If there is not enough fat in the pan, add more. Allow the roux to brown.
Catsup	1/3 cup	1 cup	
Burgundy	1/3 cup	1 cup	
Stock (preferably chicken)	1 cup	3 cups	4. Slowly add all liquids to the flour and fat mixture. Add chicken base and cayenne.
Chicken Base	2 tsp.	2 tbsp.	5. Pour over chicken in a pan and cover; bake in oven at 350°F. for 35 minutes.
Cayenne Pepper	few grains	1/4 tsp.	

BISCUIT TORTONI

(An Italian make-ahead to store in the freezer)

YIELD:	8 2-OZ. PORTIONS	24 2-OZ. PORTIONS
INGREDIENTS		
Egg Yolks	2	6
Sugar	2 tbsp.	6 tbsp.
Vanilla	1/2 tsp.	1-1/2 tsp.
OR		
Sherry	1 tsp.	1 tbsp.
Heavy Cream	1 cup	3 cups
Sugar	3 tbsp.	1/2 cup
Macaroon Crumbs	2 tbsp.	1/3 cup

METHOD

1. Combine egg yolks, sugar, and vanilla or sherry.
2. Cook in a double boiler or bain-marie, beating constantly with a wooden spoon or whip until mixture is *slightly thickened.* (If too thick, it is difficult to combine with cream.) Cool.
3. Beat cream until almost stiff. Add sugar and continue beating. When stiff (but not over-beaten), carefully fold in the egg yolk mixture.
4. Fill paper cups with mixture, using a star tube (No. 6 or 8). Top lightly with macaroon crumbs.
5. Place in deep freeze until frozen (5 to 6 hours).

Statler Club

Sunset Club

Seattle, Washington

The Sunset Club is a "she" because all of the members and almost all of the staff are "shes." And "she" has all of the nice little touches that women love—such touches as 4 china patterns and a selection of colored table linens for the private rooms, so that the hostess can coordinate her table appointments with her flowers and the theme of her party.

All of the rooms are furnished with lovely antique pieces, and there is a cozy fireplace to ward off the chill of Seattle's wet winters.

Specialties of the Northwest appear frequently on the menu with apples, salmon, and crab ranking as special favorites. The ladies in the kitchen make all of the club's pastries and desserts, as well as the fresh rolls, popovers, and hot breads which daily seduce members from their diets.

Sunset Club

POACHED SALMON FILLETS

(Salmon poached in Court Bouillon is served with a dill-flavored sauce based upon Court Bouillon)

YIELD:	10 PORTIONS	40 PORTIONS
INGREDIENTS		
Salmon	2-1/2 lb.	10 lb.
COURT BOUILLON		
Water	1 qt.	1 gal.
Carrots, Raw, chopped	1/4 cup	1 cup
Onion, sliced	1/4 cup	1 cup
Celery, chopped	1/4 cup	1 cup
Salt	1/4 tbsp.	1 tbsp.
Vinegar	1/8 cup	1/2 cup
Bay Leaf	1	4
Whole Cloves	2	8
Peppercorns	1	4
Butter	1/4 tbsp.	1 tbsp.
White Wine	1/4 cup	1 cup
EGG SAUCE		
Butter	1/2 cup	2 cups
Flour	1/2 cup	2 cups
Salt	1-1/2 tsp.	2 tbsp.
White Pepper	1/2 tsp.	2 tsp.
Court Bouillon	3 cups	12 cups
Dill Weed	1/2 tsp.	2 tsp.
OR		
Fresh Dill	1 tsp.	4 tsp.
Eggs, hard-cooked, chopped	5	20

METHOD

1. Cut 4 fillets per pound of salmon. Place in flat baking pan and cover with Court Bouillon. Cover pan with oiled or parchment paper and poach fillets gently for 10 minutes in oven at 350°F. Drain and place in buffet pan.
2. To make Court Bouillon, combine all ingredients except the wine and simmer gently for 20 to 30 minutes. Strain and add the wine. Pour over fish.
3. For a thick, well seasoned Egg Sauce, melt butter, stir in flour, salt, and pepper; gradually add strained Court Bouillon. Cook 5 minutes, then add dill weed and eggs.
4. Serve over poached salmon.

SCALLOPED OYSTERS
(Oysters the English way—baked with cream, crackers, and Worcestershire Sauce)

YIELD: INGREDIENTS	6 PORTIONS	24 PORTIONS
Cracker Crumbs, coarse	2-1/2 cups	2-1/2 qt.
Oysters, drained	1 pt.	2 qt.
Oyster Liquor	1/4 cup	1 cup
Cream	3/4 cup	3 cups
Worcestershire Sauce	1 tsp.	4 tsp.
Salt	1 tsp.	4 tsp.
Pepper	1/4 tsp.	1 tsp.
Butter, melted	1/3 cup	1-1/3 cups

METHOD
1. Arrange a third of the cracker crumbs in a well-buttered pan; cover with half of the oysters. Repeat with crumbs and oysters.
2. Blend liquids with seasonings and pour over layered crumbs and oysters. Cover with crumbs. Pour on melted butter.
3. Bake in oven at 325°F. for about 45 minutes.

APPLE CRISP ★
(An autumn treat spiced with Armagnac)

YIELD: INGREDIENTS	6 PORTIONS	24 PORTIONS
Apples, peeled, thinly sliced	2 cups	2 qt.
Cinnamon	1/2 tsp.	2 tsp.
Water	1/4 cup	1 cup
Lemon, grated rind of	1	4
Flour	3/4 cup	3 cups
Granulated Sugar	1 cup	4 cups
Salt	1/4 tsp.	1 tsp.
Butter	8 tbsp. (1/2 cup)	1 lb. (2 cups)
Heavy Cream, whipped	as needed	as needed
Armagnac	to taste	to taste

METHOD
1. Place apples in well-buttered baking dish and sprinkle with cinnamon.
2. Combine water and lemon rind and pour over apples.
3. Mix together the flour, sugar, salt, and butter and sprinkle over the apples.
4. Bake in oven at 350°F. for 30 minutes.
5. Serve hot or cold with whipped cream flavored with Armagnac or with ice cream.

★ See picture, facing page.

APPLE CRISP

The
Apple
Institute

Tamarisk Country Club

Palm Springs, California

Because Palm Springs is a resort area, and because it is located smack in the middle of the desert, almost all of its members are from out-of-state. When they make the pilgrimage to Palm Springs, they come chiefly to play golf, golf, golf, and when they come off the golf course they are generally HUNGRY. But they are also weight conscious.

With both factors in mind, the club has come up with daily menus listing such interesting items as:

- Chili and Jack Cheese Omelet garnished with Guacamole
- Peeled Apricots over Chilled Cottage Cheese topped with Sour Cream
- Apple Fritters with Canadian Bacon and Sour Cream
- Fresh Papaya stuffed with Chicken Salad and garnished with Fresh
- Strawberries
- Chicken Salad over Artichoke Bottoms garnished with Peaches and Strawberries
- Broiled Atlantic Coast Shad Roe on Toast Points, Crisp Bacon, and Creamed Spinach

The sandwich list shows an equal amount of imagination:

- The famous Reuben
- New Haven Sandwich . . . slivered baked ham on sourdough French bread, topped with cinnamon glazed apples, grilled with tangy cheddar
- Texas Burger . . . topped with homemade chili and grated cheese
- Old Vienna Burger . . . fresh ground chuck folded with egg yolks, diced onions, green peppers, and delicately seasoned

- Tamarisk Tuna Salad Sandwich . . . grilled with sliced tomatoes on French bread, accompanied by tropical fruit gelatin mold
- Golfer's Special Hamburger . . . 8 oz. of fresh ground chuck, broiled to order, creamy coleslaw, potato chips

---

COBB SALAD

(A colorful and delicious entree made famous by The Brown Derby)

YIELD:	4 PORTIONS	24 PORTIONS
INGREDIENTS		
Iceberg Lettuce	1 large head	6 heads
Watercress	1 bunch	6 bunches
Eggs, hard-cooked	3	18
Tomatoes, Medium-Sized, peeled	4	24
Avocados, Medium-Sized, peeled, pitted	2	12
Chicken Breasts, boned, cooked	2	12
Bacon Slices, cooked, crumbled	12	3 lb.
Roquefort *or* Bleu Cheese, crumbled	1/3 cup	2 cups
Chives, chopped	1 tbsp.	1/3 cup
Butter Lettuce (optional)	as needed	as needed
Olives, Radishes, Avocado Slices (optional)	to garnish	to garnish
French Dressing (optional)	as needed	as needed

METHOD

1. Using the large blade of a food chopper or a French chef's knife, coarsely chop the iceberg lettuce, watercress (without stems), eggs, tomatoes, avocados, and chicken breasts.
2. Toss with bacon, cheese, and chives.
3. Line chilled plates with butter lettuce and pile on the salad, peaking it.
4. Garnish with olives, radishes, and avocado slices.
5. Pass the dressing.

CUCUMBER SALAD WITH YOGURT DRESSING
(Mustard and cumin seeds flavor a low-calorie salad)

YIELD:

INGREDIENTS	4 to 6 PORTIONS	24 PORTIONS
Cucumbers, Medium-Sized, peeled	2	8
Mustard Seed	1/4 tsp.	1 tsp.
Cumin Seed	1/4 tsp.	1 tsp.
Yogurt	1/2 cup	2 cups
Salt	1/4 tsp.	1 tsp.
Sugar	1/4 tsp.	1 tsp.
Scallions, chopped	2	8

METHOD
1. Slice cucumbers very thin.
2. Grind mustard and cumin seeds in a mortar or whirl in a blender to crush the seeds and add to the yogurt, together with the salt and sugar.
3. Combine yogurt dressing with sliced cucumbers; top with chopped scallions.
4. Serve very cold.

GREEN GODDESS SALAD DRESSING
(Green and gorgeous—anchovy fillets are the "special" ingredients)

YIELD:

INGREDIENTS	12 PORTIONS	60 PORTIONS
Anchovy Fillets	8 to 10	50
Scallion	1	5
Parsley, minced	1/2 cup	2-1/2 cups
Fresh Tarragon	2 tbsp.	10 tbsp.
OR		
Dried Tarragon, soaked in vinegar, then strained	1 tbsp.	5 tbsp.
Chives, finely cut	1/4 cup	1-1/4 cups
Mayonnaise	3 cups	3-3/4 qt.
Tarragon Vinegar	1/4 cup	1-1/4 cups
Garlic, minced or crushed	1 clove	5 cloves

METHOD
1. Chop together anchovies and scallion until finely minced.
2. Add parsley, tarragon, and chives; mix lightly.
3. Stir in mayonnaise, vinegar, and garlic. Mix well.

SMOKED SALMON SHORTCAKE

(Rings of French toast filled with smoked salmon in a lemon cream sauce)

YIELD:

INGREDIENTS	6 PORTIONS	24 PORTIONS
Scallions, finely chopped (including tops)	3 tbsp.	3/4 cup
Celery, chopped	1/3 cup	1-1/3 cups
Butter *or* Margarine	3 tbsp.	3/4 cup (6 oz.)
Flour	1/3 cup	1-1/3 cups
Light Cream	3 cups	3 qt.
Lemon Juice	1-1/2 tsp.	2 tbsp.
Smoked Salmon, flanked	1-1/2 cups	1-1/2 qt.
Salt	to taste	to taste
Parsley, chopped	2 tbsp.	1/2 cup
French Toast Rings	12	48

METHOD

1. Cook scallions and celery in butter until soft.
2. Blend in flour.
3. Stir in cream and cook over medium heat, stirring until sauce is thick and smooth.
4. Add lemon juice and salmon.
5. Season to taste. Use caution as salmon is usually quite salty.
6. Heat 2 or 3 minutes longer; stir in parsley.
7. Spoon into French Toast Rings and serve.

SMOKED SALMON AND CREAM CHEESE OMELET

(A creamy smoked salmon sauce fills the omelet, with extra sauce on top)

YIELD:

INGREDIENTS	2 PORTIONS	24 PORTIONS
Green Onions, chopped (including tops)	2	24
Smoked Salmon, chopped	1/3 cup (3 oz.)	4 cups (36 oz.)
Butter	2 tbsp.	1-1/2 cups
Cream Cheese, cubed	3 oz.	36 oz.
Omelet (recipe, p. 232)	1 to 2 eggs	12 to 14 eggs

METHOD

1. Saute onions and salmon in butter for 2 or 3 minutes. Add cream cheese and stir until melted.
2. Fill omelet with 2 or 3 tbsp. of the sauce; serve with remaining sauce.

FRESH STRAWBERRY OMELET WITH SOUR CREAM

(A lovely brunch, lunch, or dessert—sweetened strawberries folded inside a fluffy omelet with a dollop of sour cream)

YIELD: 1 PORTION

INGREDIENTS
Fresh Strawberries, *or*
Frozen Strawberries, thawed   1/3 cup
Orange Liqueur, optional   few drops
Omelet, 2 Egg (recipe, p. 232)   1
Sugar, optional   1/2 tsp.
Sour Cream   1/3 cup
Confectioners' Sugar   1 tsp.

METHOD
1. Sweeten sliced fresh strawberries to taste, or use thawed frozen berries. Add a few drops of orange liqueur, if desired.
2. Make omelet, adding sugar to the eggs before cooking.
3. Fill omelet with strawberries and fold in half or in thirds.
4. Top with sour cream; dust with confectioners' sugar, and pass under a hot broiler just long enough to set cream.
5. Serve garnished with whole berries and mint leaves.

Tamarisk Country Club

Thorngate Country Club

Deerfield, Illinois

Thorngate Country Club is probably the only club in the world that has had much more trouble demolishing its old club than building its new one. It seems that the building the club originally purchased had at one time been a plush gambling casino. When the new club had been built nearby, and the old building was in the hands of the wrecking crew, they discovered that the large vault was built of concrete reinforced with steel bars—inside were 3 torpedo vaults. Demolition experts were lost in admiration; it was possibly the strongest vault north of Fort Knox.

Like all giants, it finally fell.

Many of the club's spur-of-the-moment improvisations have turned into club specialties, in constant demand. When an opulent Italian wedding called for myriads of jumbo stuffed mushroom caps, the thrifty Thorngate chef sauteed the sliced mushroom stems and combined them with sliced water chestnuts and bean sprouts. A popular new Thorngate vegetable dish was born.

One of the club's special salads was improvised when there had been a heavy run on the salad station, and they were almost out of greens. The chef decreed that the remaining sprigs and leaves be used as a base to be colorfully topped with marinated mushrooms, pimientos, and green peppers.

Favorite desserts at Thorngate include Hot Dutch Apple Pie. A slice of Herkimer cheese is placed on top of each wedge, and the pie is slipped into the oven to let the cheese soften and run down through the streusel-topped filling before it is served. Burgundy Wine Sherbet, Champagne Sherbet, Cinnamon Ice Cream, and Wild Blackberry Sundaes are popular, too.

THORNGATE SALAD DRESSING

(Seven different cheeses flavor this unusual dressing)

YIELD:	2 CUPS	1-1/2 GALLONS
INGREDIENTS		
Egg	1	12
Salad Oil	1-1/2 cups	9 pt.
Fresh Lemon Juice	2-1/2 tbsp.	1 pt.
Garlic, mashed	1 clove	9 cloves
Bottled Steak Sauce	1 tsp.	1/3 of 5 oz. bottle
Worcestershire Sauce	1 tsp.	1/3 of 5 oz. bottle
Parmesan, Mozzarella, "Asiento," Gruyere, New York White Cheddar, Provolone, and Longhorn Cheese	2 tsp. of each	1/2 cup of each
Liquid Hot Pepper Seasoning	3 drops	4 tsp.
Pepper	1/2 tsp.	1 tbsp.
Salt	1/2 tsp.	1 tbsp.

METHOD

Beat egg and oil together well, then blend in remaining ingredients.

Thorngate Country Club

VEAL STEAK OSKER

(Tender veal cooked in sherry then topped with crab legs, asparagus spears, and Bearnaise Sauce)

YIELD:	1 PORTION	25 PORTIONS
INGREDIENTS		
Veal Steak, 7 to 8 oz.	1	25
Butter	2 tsp.	1 cup
Shallot, Small, chopped	1	1/2 cup
Sherry	1/4 cup	6 cups
Alaska King Crab Legs	2	50
Asparagus Spears, cooked	2	50
Bearnaise Sauce	2 tbsp.	3 cups
Parsley, chopped	1 tsp.	1/2 cup
BEARNAISE SAUCE	*1 CUP*	*3 CUPS*
Shallot, chopped	1 tbsp.	3 tbsp.
Tarragon	1 tbsp.	3 tbsp.
Chervil, chopped	1 tbsp.	3 tbsp.
Thyme	sprig	3 sprigs
Bay Leaf	fragment	1
Vinegar	1/4 cup	3/4 cup
White Wine	1/4 cup	3/4 cup
Salt	pinch	1/4 tsp.
Egg Yolks	2	6
Water	1 tbsp.	3 tbsp.
Butter	1/4 lb.	3/4 lb.
Lemon Juice	squeeze	1 tsp.
Cayenne Pepper	pinch	1/8 tsp.

METHOD

1. Flatten veal steak to about 1/4 inch; saute in butter with shallots.
2. Add sherry and simmer until veal is tender. Transfer to a warm plate.
3. Top with 2 warmed crab legs and 2 asparagus spears.
4. Spoon on Bearnaise Sauce and sprinkle with chopped parsley.
5. To make Bearnaise Sauce, place shallot, tarragon, chervil, thyme, and bay leaf in a saucepan. Moisten with vinegar and wine. Season with salt. Reduce by two-thirds.
6. Allow to cool. Put in the pan the egg yolks mixed with water.
7. Beat the sauce with a whisk over very low heat. As soon as the yolks start to thicken, add the butter, little by little, beating constantly.
8. Season the sauce with lemon juice and cayenne.
9. Keep warm in a bain-marie (double boiler).

BREAST OF CHICKEN VERA CRUZ

(Marinated in sherry for 12 hours, then basted often with a flavorful oregano sauce while roasting, this dish comes to the table with rum-fried bananas and avocado slices)

YIELD:

INGREDIENTS	2 PORTIONS	24 PORTIONS
Double Breasts of Chicken, boned	2	24
Sherry	1/4 cup	3 cups
Paprika	few grains	1/4 tsp.
Oregano	few grains	1/4 tsp.
Black Pepper, freshly ground	few grains	1/4 tsp.
Salad Oil	2 tsp.	1/2 cup
Lemon Juice	2/3 tsp.	3 tbsp.
Soy Sauce	1/4 tsp.	1 tbsp.

METHOD
1. Marinate chicken breasts in sherry for 12 hours.
2. Brush with a mixture of the remaining ingredients and bake in oven at 375°F. until done, basting often.
3. Serve with bananas sauteed in rum and butter and with sliced avocado.

POTATO PUFFS EMMENTHALER ★

(Emmenthaler cheese and ham flavor crisp deep-fried potato balls)

YIELD:

INGREDIENTS	5 PORTIONS	25 PORTIONS
Idaho Potatoes, finely grated	2 to 3	13
Baking Powder	1/2 tsp.	2-1/2 tsp.
Flour	1/3 cup	1-2/3 cups
Salt	1/2 tsp.	1 tbsp.
White Pepper	1/4 tsp.	1-1/4 tsp.
Egg, beaten	1	5
Emmenthaler *or* Swiss Cheese, grated	3 tbsp.	7 to 8 oz.
Ham, cut in small dice	3 tbsp.	7 to 8 oz.
Parsley, chopped	1 tsp.	2 tbsp.
Peanut Oil	as needed	as needed

METHOD
1. Combine all ingredients except peanut oil. Drop 1-inch round balls into peanut oil which has been heated to 350°F. Fry until a golden brown; drain.
2. Finish in oven at 375°F. for 10 minutes.

★ See picture, facing page.

POTATO PUFFS EMMENTHALER

Peanut
Associates,
Inc.

UNUSUAL CHICKEN BREADING
(Stone-ground flour and stone-ground corn meal give fried chicken "character")

YIELD:	4 SERVINGS	24 SERVINGS	
INGREDIENTS			METHOD
Chicken, cut up for frying	2	12	Dip chicken pieces in a mixture of egg and buttermilk, then into combined dry ingredients; saute in butter.
Eggs	2	12	
Buttermilk	1/4 cup	1-1/2 cups	
Stone-Ground Flour	1/2 cup	3/4 lb. (3 cups)	
Stone-Ground Corn Meal	1/2 cup	1 lb. (3 cups)	
Rolled Corn Flakes	1/4 cup	1-1/2 cups	
Salt	2 tsp.	2 tbsp.	
Pepper	1/2 tsp.	1 tbsp.	
Butter	as needed	as needed	

SAGE STUFFING FOR WALLEYED PIKE
(An elegant low-cost addition to any buffet)

YIELD:	FOR 1 FISH	METHOD
INGREDIENTS		1. Brush body cavity of fish (do not use fillets) with dry vermouth. Combine next 5 ingredients and spoon into body cavity.
Walleyed Pike	1 5-lb. fish	
Dry Vermouth	as needed	2. Sprinkle fish with paprika, dot with butter, and bake in oven at 350°F., allowing 5 to 10 minutes per pound.
Bread Cubes, soft	2 cups	
Onion, finely diced	2 tbsp.	
Celery, finely diced	2 tbsp.	
Dried Sage	1/8 tsp.	
OR		
Fresh Sage	1/4 tsp.	
Egg, beaten	1	
Paprika	as needed	
Butter	2 tbsp.	

Union League Club

Philadelphia, Pennsylvania

The founding of the Union League Club in 1862 was inspired by patriotism and devotion to the preservation of the Union during the Civil War. Today, the club is a storehouse of priceless information on Abraham Lincoln and the Civil War, as well as on the Republican Party.

The club is housed in a downtown building which was built in 1865. Later additions expanded the building to an entire city block with a staff of more than 300 people.

The Memorial Room, with its statue of Abraham Lincoln and fine collection of books written about Lincoln and the Civil War, is of great scholarly interest. Among the collection are the shorthand notes and transcription of the interrogation at the time of Lincoln's assassination. Another of the club's treasures is one of the few remaining original copies of the Emancipation Proclamation.

The main dining rooms are called North and South Marble, and that aptly describes the decor. The center of interest on each table is a pressed glass relish dish holding a Union League mixture of chili sauce, India relish, Tabasco sauce, and Worcestershire sauce. Assorted crackers and melba toast are available for transporting this appetite-building mixture by hand to mouth.

Change is not the order of the day at the Union League, and one of the institutions no one would ever tamper with is the New Year's Day stag reception and open house. Fishhouse Punch and a buffet help to kill the pain from the night before. The punch is an effective combination of blended whiskey, Jamaica rum, Champagne, peach brandy, orange and lemon juices—combined and cut with soda. Members force their medicine down like good soldiers.

OLD-FASHIONED FRIZZLED BEEF WITH CREAM BROWN SAUCE

(This old favorite can stand alone or be served with toast, noodles, an omelette, waffles or crepes)

YIELD:

INGREDIENTS	6 PORTIONS	24 PORTIONS
Butter	3 tbsp.	3/4 cup
Flour	4 tbsp.	1 cup
Cream	1-1/3 cups	5-1/3 cups
Milk	2/3 cup	2-2/3 cups
Paprika	to color	to color
Dried Beef, thinly sliced	9 oz.	2-1/4 lb.

METHOD

1. Make a roux by melting butter in pan and stirring in flour. Brown the roux slightly.
2. Slowly add cream and milk, stirring constantly to keep the mixture smooth.
3. Add paprika and dried beef; cook for 5 minutes.
4. Serve in casserole with toast points; with buttered noodles; with an omelette; with waffles, or as a filling for crepes.

DEVILED CRAB

(Deep-fried crab with a strong hint of English mustard)

YIELD:

INGREDIENTS	6 PORTIONS	24 PORTIONS
Onion, medium dice	3 tbsp.	3/4 cup
Butter	1/4 lb.	1 lb.
Flour	2 tbsp.	1/2 cup
Cream	1 cup	1 qt.
Lump Crabmeat	1 can (14 oz.)	4-1/2 lb.
Worcestershire Sauce	1/2 tsp.	2 tsp.
English Mustard	1/2 tsp.	2 tsp.
Salt	1/2 tsp.	2 tsp.
White Pepper	1/4 tsp.	1 tsp.
Egg Yolks	2	8
Bread Crumbs	1 cup	1 qt.
Fat for Deep Frying	as needed	as needed

METHOD

1. Saute onion in butter until transparent; add flour to thicken; stir in cream, cooking until thick.
2. Add lump crabmeat. Season with Worcestershire sauce, English mustard, salt, and pepper.
3. Gently stir in egg yolks; avoid breaking crabmeat.
4. Allow to cool. Form mixture into small cakes. Bread and cook in deep fat at 350 to 400°F. until brown; finish off in oven at 300°F. for about 15 minutes.

CRABMEAT DEWEY

(Sherry and mushrooms flavor crabmeat in a rich Newburg Sauce)

YIELD:	6 PORTIONS	24 PORTIONS
INGREDIENTS		
NEWBURG SAUCE		
Butter	3 tbsp.	3/4 cup
Flour	3 tbsp.	3/4 cup
Light Cream	1 qt.	4 qt.
Sherry	1/3 cup	1-1/3 cups
CRABMEAT DEWEY		
Newburg Sauce	1 qt.	1 gal.
Pimiento, diced	1	4
Mushrooms, diced	6	24
Egg Shade *or* Yellow Food Coloring	2 to 3 tsp.	2 to 3 tbsp.
Lump Crabmeat	1 lb.	4 lb.
Salt	to taste	to taste
Pepper	to taste	to taste

METHOD

1. For the Newburg Sauce, melt butter and stir in flour. Gradually add cream. Simmer for five minutes. Add sherry.
2. To make Crabmeat Dewey, heat Newburg Sauce; add pimiento and mushrooms; simmer; add coloring. At the last minute add crabmeat, salt, pepper, and additional sherry, if desired.
3. Serve on rice or toast points or in individual shells.

Union League Club

Valencia Club

New Orleans, Louisiana

The Valencia Club was founded in 1948 by a group of parents in answer to a need for a supervised recreational center for high school children. It is located in the heart of New Orleans and offers worthwhile learning experiences such as dressmaking and art, athletic, artistic, card, and chess competitions, as well as just plain recreation.

The club measures the success of a party in the tons of catsup served, not in pounds of prime rib. A thousand teenagers full of ideas might sound like a parents' nightmare, but pity (or envy) the chef who has to fill those yawning caverns.

BAKED GRITS

(A breakfast favorite in the South, grits and Cheddar cheese are delicious with ham or sausage)

YIELD:	6 PORTIONS	24 PORTIONS
INGREDIENTS		
Grits	1 cup	1 qt.
Water, boiling	2 cups	2 qt.
Salt	1 tsp.	4 tsp.
Milk	1 cup	1 qt.
Butter	4 tbsp. (1/4 cup)	1/2 lb. (1 cup)
Red Pepper	few grains	1/4 tsp.
Egg Yolks, beaten	2	8
Cheddar Cheese, grated	1 cup	1 lb. (qt.)
Paprika	as needed	as needed

METHOD

1. Cook grits in boiling water for 5 minutes.
2. Add salt and milk and cook together over moderate heat for 15 minutes.
3. Stir in butter, red pepper, and egg yolks.
4. Pour mixture into buttered casserole. Top with grated cheese. Sprinkle with paprika. Bake in oven at 350°F. for about 45 minutes, or until solid.

SHRIMP-BAKED EGGPLANT

(Shrimp and eggplant baked with a whiff of garlic)

YIELD:	3 PORTIONS	24 PORTIONS
INGREDIENTS		
Eggplant, peeled	1	8
Butter	1-1/2 tsp.	2 oz. (1/4 cup)
Bell Pepper	1/4	2
Onion, minced	1/4	2
Celery, sliced	1/2 rib	4 ribs
Shrimp, cleaned, deveined	1/4 lb.	2 lbs.
Bread Crumbs, seasoned	1/4 pkg. (3 oz.)	1-1/2 lb.
Parsley, chopped	2 tbsp.	1 cup
Garlic, pressed	1/2 clove	4 cloves
Butter	1 tbsp.	4 oz. (1/2 cup)

METHOD

1. Cut eggplant into large pieces and boil until tender; drain and set aside both eggplant and water.
2. Saute pepper, onion, and celery in butter until slightly browned.
3. Add shrimp and cook for 5 minutes.
4. Mix in and cook for 15 to 20 minutes the cooked eggplant, 3/4 of the bread crumbs, and the parsley and garlic. If mixture is too dry, add eggplant stock.
5. Pour into buttered baking dish; sprinkle with remaining bread crumbs and dot with butter. Bake in oven at 350°F. until brown, about 45 minutes.

Wichita Country Club

Wichita, Kansas

A favorite way of serving prime Kansas beef at the Wichita Country Club is browning whole tenderloin or sirloin strips in the broiler and allowing them to cool. Just before serving time, the strip is brushed with prepared French mustard, sprinkled with dark brown sugar, and finished off in a hot oven. The mustard and sugar caramelize and have an apparent tenderizing effect on the already tender meat. The beef is flambeed with brandy when served at the table.

Second in popularity to beef is lamb. A whole young lamb, roasted, is featured on the club's weekly buffet. The lamb is sprinkled with salt, pepper, and rosemary. While roasting, it is liberally basted with beer. Members are "crazy about it."

Another club favorite, but one that is reserved for banquets or special parties, is Wichita Roman Punch in Orange Surprise. The cup is the "surprise." To produce it, a circular cut is made barely through the skin of an orange, about two-thirds of the distance from the bottom. A teaspoon is inserted between the skin and the membrane, the orange is rotated, and the spoon loosens the skin from the membrane which encloses the pulp without tearing the membrane. The process is repeated on the other portion of the orange, and the whole fruit emerges from the shell intact. The top third of the skin is then sliced about one-fourth inch from the first cut. This quarter-inch ring is used as a base upon which to set the filled bottom of the orange. The punch is a combination of lemon and orange fruit juice bases, white wine, and a little rum, frozen to a slush and mixed with brandied cherries.

QUICHE LORRAINE

(Bacon in the bottom adds extra flavor to a Swiss favorite)

YIELD:	1 9-INCH PIE	4 9-INCH PIES	METHOD
INGREDIENTS			1. Line pie plate with tender pastry.
Pastry Shell	1	4	2. Cut bacon slices in half; broil and drain.
Bacon	6 thick slices	24 thick slices	3. Cover the pie crust with overlapping slices of bacon and cheese.
Swiss *or* Gruyere Cheese	12 thin slices	48 thin slices	4. Beat together the eggs, flour, nutmeg, salt, and cayenne. Add the cream and melted butter.
Eggs	4	16 (4 cups)	
Flour	1 tbsp.	1/4 cup	5. Pour the custard over the bacon and cheese. Bake quiche in oven at 370°F. for about 40 minutes, or until custard is set and the top nicely browned. Best served warm.
Nutmeg	generous grating	generous grating	
Salt	1/2 tsp	2 tsp.	
Cayenne Pepper	few grains	1/8 tsp.	
Light Cream	2 cups	8 cups	
Butter, melted, cooled	1-1/2 tbsp.	12 oz. (6 tbsp.)	

SHERRIED QUAIL

(Tender little quail served with a tart sherry sauce)

YIELD:	4 PORTIONS	24 PORTIONS	METHOD
INGREDIENTS			1. Sprinkle quail with salt and paprika.
Quail	4	24	2. Saute in butter until brown. Cover tightly and cook slowly for 1 hour (longer for older birds). Then remove birds and keep hot.
Salt	to taste	to taste	
Paprika	to taste	to taste	
Butter	1-1/2 tbsp.	1/4 lb. (8 tbsp.)	3. Pour in sherry, lemon juice, and Worcestershire sauce and cook until partially reduced.
Sherry	1/4 cup	1-1/2 cup	4. Thicken with flour combined with cream. Cook until thick and bubbly; serve with the quail.
Lemon, juice of	1/2	3	
Worcestershire Sauce	1-1/2 tsp.	3 tbsp.	
Flour	1/2 tbsp.	3 tbsp.	
Heavy Cream	1/2 cup	3 cups	

GOURMET CASSEROLE OF CHICKEN BREAST

(The breasts are flambeed with Curacao before simmering with pineapple juice, Chablis, and flavorings, but orange is the principle flavor)

YIELD:	4 PORTIONS	24 PORTIONS

INGREDIENTS			METHOD
Chicken Breasts	2	12	1. Saute the breasts in butter until golden brown.
Butter	2 tbsp.	6 oz. (3/4 cup)	2. Sprinkle orange peel, salt, and pepper over the breasts.
Orange Peel, grated	1 tbsp.	(6 tbsp.)	3. Flambe with Curacao.
Salt	to taste	to taste	4. Stir in cornstarch which has been mixed with water.
Pepper	to taste	to taste	
Curacao	1 tbsp.	3 oz.	5. Gradually add pineapple juice, Chablis, Worcestershire sauce and liquid hot pepper seasoning; simmer for 10 to 15 minutes to reduce to a medium consistency.
Cornstarch	1/2 tsp.	3 tsp.	
Pineapple Juice	1/4 cup	12 oz. (1-1/2 cups)	
Chablis	1/4 cup	12 oz. (1-1/2 cups)	6. Before serving, add a little more grated orange peel and a sprinkle of Grand Marnier.
Worcestershire Sauce	dash	a few drops	7. Serve in individual casseroles on a bed of hot rice.
Liquid Hot Pepper Seasoning	dash	a few drops	
Grand Marnier	sprinkle	sprinkle	
Rice, cooked	as needed	as needed	

CREPES SOUFFLE GRAND MARNIER

YIELD:	6 PORTIONS	24 PORTIONS
INGREDIENTS		
CREPES		
Eggs, slightly beaten	1-1/2	6
Milk	2 tbsp	1/2 cup
Flour	2-1/4 tsp.	3 tbsp.
Salt	1/8 tsp.	1/2 tsp.
Butter, melted	1 tbsp.	2 oz. (4 tbsp.)
PASTRY CREAM		
Egg Yolk	1	4
Granulated Sugar	1-1/2 tbsp.	6 tbsp.
Flour	1-1/2 tbsp.	6 tbsp.
Cornstarch	1/4 tsp.	1 tsp.
Milk, scalded	1/2 cup	2 cups
Butter	1 tsp.	1 tbsp.
Grand Marnier	1/2 tbsp.	2 tbsp.
FILLING		
Egg White	1	4
Sugar	1/2 tbsp.	2 tbsp.
Cream of Tartar	omit	pinch
Sugar	1 tsp.	1 tbsp.

METHOD

1. To make Crepes, combine eggs, milk, flour, and salt until smooth.
2. Add melted butter and stir.
3. Cover bottom of small heated skillet with butter and then with batter. Cook over medium heat until light brown on both sides, turning once. These can be made ahead and frozen.
4. To make Pastry Cream, stir egg yolks, sugar, flour, and cornstarch in a saucepan and mix thoroughly.
5. Gradually stir in scalded milk. Stir over medium heat until cream is smooth and thick (about 3 minutes).
6. Remove from heat.
7. Add butter and stir occasionally as mixture cools. Stir in Grand Marnier.
8. For Filling, beat together egg whites, sugar, and cream of tartar.
9. Fold egg white mixture into Pastry Cream.
10. Fill each of the crepes with 2 tbsp. of the mixture.
11. Fold ends over and arrange on platter.
12. Sprinkle with 1 tbsp. sugar and bake in hot oven for 10 minutes. Serve immediately.

Woodmont Country Club

Rockville, Maryland

Opulence, quality, and lots of eye appeal are of prime importance at the Woodmont Country Club. Here they do such extras as sculpturing mushrooms to garnish steaks, frosting grapes for fruit plates, scooping balls out of a pale honeydew or Persian melon and inserting bright balls of watermelon in their place, and serving fresh fruit as an appetizer in a basket made of a grapefruit shell.

Among the popular hors d'oeuvre items are very thin turnip slices, left in cold water so that they will curve and cup to serve as crisp little holders for yellow cheese. Sliced salami, lightly fried, cups in the same manner and makes another appetizing appetizer when you fill it with a cheese or dip. Cherry tomatoes often are stuffed with pate, and Phoenix wings (the upper part of the chicken wing) are fried in deep fat, sprinkled with a seasoned salt, and served hot.

At Woodmont, the lounge area is stocked with crisp celery and carrot sticks at cocktail time, as well as with nuts, crackers, and a good cheese spread made by whipping New York cheddar to an easy spreading consistency with dry vermouth.

SWEET AND SOUR CHICKEN

(Batter-fried chicken cubes served with pineapple chunks in a sweet and sour sauce)

YIELD:	6 PORTIONS	24 PORTIONS
INGREDIENTS		
Chicken	2-1/2 lb.	10 lb.
Salt	to taste	to taste
Pepper	to taste	to taste
Flour	3 tbsp.	3/4 cup
Cornstarch	1 tbsp.	1/4 cup
Egg, beaten	1	4
Salad Oil	2 tsp.	3 tbsp.
Water	3 tbsp.	3/4 cup
Cooking Oil	as needed	as needed
SWEET AND SOUR SAUCE		
Pineapple Chunks	1 No. 2 can	10 cups
Vinegar	3/4 cup	3 cups
Catsup	2 tbsp.	1/2 cup
Salt	to taste	to taste
Cornstarch	3 tbsp.	3/4 cup
Sugar	1-1/2 cups	6 cups
Water	1/2 cup	2 cups

METHOD

1. Wash, clean, skin, and bone chicken; cut into 1-inch cubes. Season with salt and pepper.
2. Prepare batter, stirring together flour and cornstarch. Add egg, salad oil, and water.
3. Dip chicken cubes in batter to coat well. Fry cubes in deep fat at 350°F. until golden brown. Drain and serve with Sweet and Sour Sauce.
4. To make Sweet and Sour Sauce, place in saucepan and bring to a full boil 1/2 of the pineapple chunks and 1/2 of their liquid and all of the vinegar, catsup, and salt.
5. Combine cornstarch with sugar and stir in cold water; add to pineapple mixture and cook until thickened.
6. Combine sauce with chicken and pineapple chunks.

BAKED SHRIMP WITH CRABMEAT

(Shrimp piled high with crabmeat makes a popular appetizer)

YIELD:	6 PORTIONS	24 PORTIONS
INGREDIENTS		
Shrimp, Large, cooked	12	48
Butter	1/4 cup	1 cup
STUFFING		
Crabmeat	1 lb.	4 lb.
Bread Crumbs, fine	2 tbsp.	1/2 cup
Onion, minced	1/2 cup	2 cups
Butter	1 tbsp.	1/4 cup
Parsley, minced	1 tbsp.	1/4 cup
Liquid Hot Pepper Seasoning	dash	1/8 tsp.
Worcestershire Sauce	1/4 tsp.	1 tsp.
Salt	1/2 tsp.	2 tsp.
White Pepper	1/8 tsp.	1/2 tsp.
Egg, beaten	1	4
Paprika	as needed	as needed
Butter, melted	2 tbsp.	1/2 cup

METHOD

1. Shell, devein, and butterfly the shrimp (so each will lie flat, all in one piece). Place shrimp on greased pan; brush with melted butter.
2. To make Stuffing, lightly mix together: crabmeat, bread crumbs, onion sauteed in butter, parsley, liquid hot pepper seasoning, Worcestershire, salt, pepper, and egg.
3. Place stuffing in mounds on each shrimp. Sprinkle each mound with paprika and butter.
4. Bake in pre-heated oven at 500°F. for 8 to 10 minutes.

Woodmont Country Club

The Woodstock Club

Indianapolis, Indiana

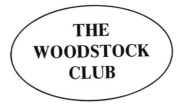

Many people when they see the Woodstock Country Club for the first time ask, "Whose home was this originally?" Built originally as a clubhouse, the rambling building constructed in 1915, is a modular jigsaw puzzle with mellow, understated charm.

Opened primarily as a tennis club, the club has added golf and a pool to its facilities. But the club's setting along the White River is enough to bring anyone to the club in summer, and its crackling fireplaces draw members even when the weather is inhospitable. The lounge, a long room with a two-story ceiling, has its length broken by a balcony renowned in Indianapolis for the number of bridal bouquets tossed over the grillwork.

Woodstock's staff makes all of the pastries and desserts the club serves, and most of the breads. The menu features good midwestern standbys. Every time a new item such as "sea squab" is listed on the menu, the manager has to explain to members that it is actually the tail of the blowfish. The "squab" has a sweet, firm meat and, when deep fried, it makes a good low-cost filler for buffets.

HOT GERMAN POTATO SALAD

(A midwestern favorite that goes especially well with beef or ham)

YIELD:	5 PORTIONS	20 PORTIONS
INGREDIENTS		
Potatoes, Medium-Sized	9	36
Water	1 cup	1 qt.
Sugar	1/4 cup	1 cup
Celery Seed	1 tbsp.	1/4 cup
Vinegar	1 cup	1 qt.
Salt	1/8 cup	1/2 cup
Bacon, diced	1/4 lb.	1 lb.
Flour	1-1/2 tbsp.	1/3 cup
Eggs, hard-cooked	2	10
Onion, grated	2 tbsp.	1/2 cup
Parsley, chopped	2 tbsp.	1/2 cup

METHOD
1. Peel, boil, and slice potatoes.
2. Bring next 5 ingredients to a boil.
3. Brown bacon; remove from pan. Add flour to the bacon drippings to make a roux. Add the cooked liquid until mixture is of medium thickness.
4. Mix potatoes with the sauce.
5. Garnish with sliced egg, grated onion, diced cooked bacon, and chopped parsley. (Onion can be added to the sauce.)

PUREED PEAS ON ARTICHOKE BOTTOMS

(A glamorous vegetable preparation that can be used as garniture)

YIELD:	7 to 9 BOTTOMS	24 BOTTOMS
INGREDIENTS		
Peas, Frozen	1 8-oz. pkg.	24 oz.
Onion, Small, diced	1	3
Salt	to taste	to taste
Pepper	to taste	to taste
Artichoke Bottoms, Canned	1 can, 7-3/4 oz.	3 cans, 7-3/4 oz.

METHOD
1. Cook frozen peas as directed. Drain and reserve cooking water. While they are still hot, put peas into blender with some diced onion. Fill blender only half full and blend, using a little of the water the peas were cooked in or using cream (the puree must not be too thin). Repeat until all peas are pureed.
2. Season to taste with salt and pepper.
3. Drain canned artichoke bottoms and steam until hot. Using a pastry bag, swirl puree on top of each artichoke bottom. Reheat in oven just before serving.

Note   Puree may be made ahead and can be frozen.

BOSC PEAR EN SABAYON

(Poached pears stuffed with chestnuts awash in a sea of Sabayon)

YIELD:	6 PORTIONS	24 PORTIONS
INGREDIENTS		
Bosc Pears	6	24
Marrons Debris	6	24
or		
Whole Marrons		
SABAYON SAUCE		
Egg Yolks	6	24
Granulated Sugar	2/3 cup	2-2/3 cups
Almond-Flavored		
Marsala	1 cup	1 qt.
Rum	1 tbsp.	2 oz.
		(1/4 cup)

METHOD

1. Select Bosc pears that are free of blemishes and, preferably, with the stem intact. Peel and core pears, leaving a small amount of skin next to the stem. Poach pears until barely done.

2. Place marrons debris or whole marrons in the core cavities and set each poached pear upright in serving dish; pour Sabayon Sauce around the pear.

3. To make Sabayon Sauce, whip together egg yolks and sugar. Stir in the Marsala. Cook in top of double boiler, starting over cold water. Stir until water reaches the boiling point or until the mixture is thick and creamy. Add rum. Serve hot.

Note Woodstock also uses a warm peach half, cut side down, with Sabayon Sauce when pears are unobtainable. It is attractive served in a champagne glass.

GATEAU RICHE ★

(Almond cookies, molded to champagne glasses, make a nest for chocolate sauce, ice cream, and coffee-flavored whipped cream)

YIELD: INGREDIENTS	15 PORTIONS	60 PORTIONS
Almonds, finely ground	3 tbsp.	3/4 cup
Butter, unsalted	2 tbsp.	1/2 cup
Cream	2-1/2 tsp.	2 tbsp.
Sugar	2 tbsp.	1/2 cup
Flour	8 tsp.	10 tbsp.
Chocolate Syrup	as needed	as needed
Ice Cream	as needed	as needed
Coffee Whipped Cream*	as needed	as needed

METHOD

1. Combine all ingredients in a small heavy pan; cook and stir until butter melts. Arrange by tablespoons 3-inches apart on well-buttered and floured cookie sheets. Spread out to cup size with finger tips. Bake in oven at 350°F. for about 7 minutes, until delicately brown around the edges but still bubbling slightly in the center.

2. Let cool 1 minute, until edges are firm enough to lift with a spatula. Place inside champagne glasses while hot so the gateaus (cakes) will mold to the shape of the glass. They are brittle when cool.

3. To serve, add a tablespoon of your best chocolate syrup, then a scoop of extra rich ice cream. Garnish with coffee whipped cream.

*Woodstock adds powdered decaffeinated coffee to sweetened whipped cream. The cream is a light tan color and can be piped from a pastry bag. Serve plain or garnish with gateau crumbs.

★ See picture, facing page.

GATEAU RICHE

Recipe References

BORDELAISE SAUCE

YIELD: 2 CUPS

INGREDIENTS

BROWN SAUCE

Butter	3 tbsp.
Flour	4 tbsp.
Beef Stock, boiling	1 cup

BORDELAISE

Shallots, minced	2 tbsp.
Butter	1 tbsp.
Red Wine	1/2 cup
Thyme	pinch
Pepper	pinch
Bay Leaf, Powdered	pinch
Salt	to taste
Beef Marrow, diced, poached 3 minutes in boiling liquid	1/3 cup

METHOD

BROWN SAUCE

1. Combine butter and flour in saucepan over low heat, stirring constantly for 8 to 10 minutes, until the mixture turns a golden color.
2. Blend in boiling stock, stirring constantly.

BORDELAISE

1. Saute shallots in butter, but do not brown. Add wine and seasonings; boil until reduced by 1/2.
2. Add Brown Sauce and simmer until lightly thickened (3 to 4 minutes).
3. Fold in the marrow.

CHAUDFROID SAUCE

YIELD: 2 CUPS

INGREDIENTS

Butter	2 tbsp.
Flour	2 tbsp.
Chicken Broth, hot	1 cup
Salt	pinch
Gelatine, Unflavored	1 envelope (1 oz.)
Water	2-1/2 tbsp.
Heavy Cream	1/2 cup

METHOD

1. Combine butter and flour in a saucepan over low heat for 2 minutes.
2. Gradually stir in the chicken broth, beating until the sauce is smooth and thickened.
3. Add the salt; cook over low heat for 30 minutes; strain.
4. Stir in the gelatine, which has been softened in the water. Add the cream and stir well.

CREAMY VELOUTE SAUCE

YIELD: 2 CUPS

INGREDIENTS		METHOD
Butter	1 tbsp.	
Flour	1-1/2 tbsp.	
Salt	1/8 tsp.	
Milk	1 cup	
Chicken *or* Fish Stock	1 cup	
Salt	to taste	
Pepper	to taste	

METHOD

1. In a saucepan over low heat, melt butter and blend in flour; stir for 2 minutes; do not allow the roux to color. Remove from heat.
2. Add salt to milk and stock; bring to a boil. Beating constantly, slowly pour boiling liquid into roux. Place over medium heat and boil for 1 minute, stirring constantly. Remove from heat and add seasonings.

CREAM SAUCE OR BECHAMEL

YIELD: 3/4 CUP

INGREDIENTS

Butter	2 tbsp.
Flour	1-1/2 tbsp.
Milk	3/4 cup
Onion, Small	1
Whole Clove	1
Bay Leaf	1/3
Salt	to taste

METHOD

1. In a heavy saucepan, melt the butter and stir in flour; slowly stir in milk, using a wire whisk to prevent lumping.
2. Add onion, whole clove, and bay leaf; cook and stir until sauce is thick and smooth and there is no taste of starch. (Once the sauce has come to the boiling point it can be cooked in the oven for 20 minutes.)
3. Remove onion, whole clove, and bay leaf; season to taste.

HOLLANDAISE SAUCE

YIELD: 1 CUP

INGREDIENTS   METHOD

Egg Yolks	4
Butter	1/2 cup
Lemon Juice	2 to 3 tsp.
Salt	dash
White Pepper	dash
Nutmeg	few grains

VARIATIONS: Double Hollandaise (double egg yolks); Mock Hollandaise (half Veloute or Cream Sauce); Mousseline (half whipped cream); Maltaise (grated orange peel and some concentrated orange juice); Figaro (tomato puree and poached fine julienne of celery added); Grimod (saffron added)

1. Place egg yolks and 1/3 of the butter in top of double boiler. Do not let water in bottom of double boiler touch top pan. Cook over hot, not boiling, water until butter melts, stirring rapidly.
2. Add 1/3 more of the butter and continue stirring. As mixture thickens and butter melts, add remaining butter, stirring constantly. When butter is melted, remove pan from hot water; stir rapidly 2 minutes longer.
3. Stir in lemon juice a teaspoon at a time; add seasonings.
4. Heat again over hot water, stirring constantly until thickened, 2 to 3 minutes. Remove from heat at once. If sauce curdles, immediately beat in 1 to 2 tablespoons boiling water.

POULET SAUCE

YIELD: 2 CUPS

INGREDIENTS
Butter	1-1/2 tbsp.
Flour	2 tbsp.
Chicken Stock	3/4 cup
Mushrooms, sliced or chopped	1 cup
Egg Yolk	1
Heavy Cream	1/4 cup
Salt	to taste
Pepper	to taste
Sweet Basil	1/4 tsp.

METHOD

1. Combine butter and flour in saucepan over low heat for 2 minutes. Remove this roux from heat.
2. Slowly add strained stock to the roux, beating with a wire whip to blend smoothly. Stirring constantly, boil for 1 minute. Sauce will be very thick. Stir in mushrooms.
3. Blend the egg yolk and cream together and gradually beat in the hot sauce, in a thin stream. Pour the sauce back into the saucepan. Stir over medium high heat until the sauce comes to a boil. Boil 1 minute, stirring constantly. Remove from heat and add seasonings.

The Army and Navy Club

(See pages 1 to 8 for description of club and recipes.)

MADEIRA SAUCE

YIELD: 2-1/2 CUPS

INGREDIENTS

BROWN SAUCE

Butter	3 tbsp.
Flour	4 tbsp.
Stock, boiling	1-1/2 cups

MADEIRA

Madeira	1/2 cup
Parsley	1 sprig
Bay Leaf, Powdered	pinch
Thyme	1/4 tsp.
Salt	to taste
Pepper	to taste
Butter, softened	2 to 3 tbsp.

METHOD

BROWN SAUCE

1. Combine butter and flour in saucepan over low heat, stirring constantly for 8 to 10 minutes, until the mixture turns a golden color.
2. Blend in boiling stock, stirring constantly.

MADEIRA

1. Combine wine and seasonings in saucepan and boil hard until mixture has reduced to about 3 tbsp.
2. Add Brown Sauce and simmer 1 to 2 minutes. If more wine is needed, add it slowly.
3. Remove from heat; just before serving, beat in butter, a small amount at a time.

Concordia-Argonaut Club

(See pages 28 to 30 for description of club and recipes.)

MUSHROOM SAUCE

YIELD: 2 CUPS

INGREDIENTS
Garlic	1/2 clove
Butter	2 tbsp.
Fresh Mushrooms, sliced	1/4 lb.
Flour	2 tbsp.
Bouillon*	1 cup
Salt	to taste
Pepper	to taste
Lemon Juice *or* Sherry, optional	to taste

*Canned bouillon may be used or add 2 bouillon cubes to 1 cup of boiling water and stir to dissolve.

METHOD
1. Rub bottom of saucepan with garlic and discard clove. Melt butter and saute mushrooms.
2. Remove mushrooms and stir in flour; when well blended, gradually add bouillon. Stir constantly until mixture reaches the boiling point and season to taste. Add the mushrooms and serve hot.

LEMON SAUCE

YIELD: 2 CUPS

INGREDIENTS
Granulated Sugar	1 cup
Cornstarch	2 tbsp.
Water	2 cups
Lemon, juice and grated rind of	1
Butter	3 tbsp.
Orange-Flavored Liqueur	2 tsp.

METHOD
1. In a saucepan, stir together sugar and cornstarch; slowly stir in water. Bring to a boil over low heat and cook for 8 minutes, stirring constantly.
2. Stir in lemon juice and rind, butter, and liqueur; serve hot. The sauce can be made ahead and warmed in a double boiler.

HOT BUTTERED RUM SAUCE

YIELD: 2 CUPS

INGREDIENTS   METHOD
Sugar   1 cup   Boil sugar and water together for 5 minutes.
Water   2/3 cup   Add rum and butter and remove from heat.
Rum, Light *or* Medium   1/4 cup
Butter   1/4 cup

Note
Dark rum may be used in lesser quantity, if it is
flambeed to burn off the alcohol.

VANILLA PUDDING

YIELD: 2 CUPS   3 QT.
INGREDIENTS   METHOD
Sugar   1/4 cup   1-1/2 cups   1. Combine sugar, cornstarch, and salt in the
Cornstarch   3 tbsp.   1 cup,   top of a double boiler; gradually stir in
                               2 tbsp.   milk and stir until mixture begins to thick-
Salt   1/8 tsp.   3/4 tsp.   en (8 to 12 minutes). Cover and continue
Milk   2 cups   3 qt.   to cook 10 minutes longer.
Egg, beaten   1   6   2. Stir some of the hot mixture into the egg(s),
Vanilla   1/2 tsp.   1 tbsp.   then stir egg mixture into milk mixture and
                                              combine well. Cook 2 minutes, stirring
                                              constantly. Do not overcook; the pudding
                                              will thicken more as it cools. Remove from
                                              heat.
                                           3. When slightly cooled, stir in vanilla.

PUFF PASTE

YIELD: 2 LB.

INGREDIENTS

All-purpose *or* Bread Flour	1 lb.
Salt	pinch
Butter	3 tbsp.
Egg	1
Water, cold	1/2 cup
Butter	1 lb.

Note

Puff paste dough keeps extremely well in the re-frigerator, and even longer in the freezer.

METHOD

1. Using electric mixer, combine flour, salt, 3 tbsp. butter, egg, and cold water. Shape into a ball and let stand 15 to 20 minutes.
2. Knead the second amount of butter until it is the same consistency as the dough; it will be difficult to handle if one is stiffer than the other.
3. Roll dough into a large square, leaving the center somewhat thicker. Place kneaded butter in the center, patting it to an even thickness. Bring the 4 corners of the pastry up over the dough and seal.
4. Flatten with a rolling pin by gently pounding dough. Roll out about 1/2-inch thick and twice as long as it is wide.
5. Fold both ends toward the middle and double again. Wrap in plastic and refrigerate for 20 to 30 minutes.
6. Repeat steps 4 and 5 four times.

Missouri Athletic Club

(See pages 137 to 139 for description of club and recipes.)

PLAIN OMELET

YIELD: 1 to 2 PORTIONS

INGREDIENTS   METHOD

Eggs   2 or 3   1. Beat eggs and seasonings in a mixing bowl
Salt   pinch   until whites and yolks are just blended.
Pepper   pinch   2. Place the butter in an omelet pan and set
Butter   1 tbsp.   over high heat. Tilt the pan to coat all sides
                                   with butter. Pour in eggs.
                               3. Slide pan back and forth rapidly over the
                                   heat, stirring lightly with a fork. In 3 to 4
                                   seconds the eggs will become a light custard.
                                   (A filling would go in at this point.)
                               4. Lift the handle of the pan at a 45-degree
                                   angle over the heat and gather eggs at the
                                   far lip of the pan with the back of the fork.
                                   Run the fork around the lip of the pan to
                                   loosen the omelet.
                               5. Slide the omelet onto a heated plate, fold-
                                   ing it in half or thirds as it comes from the
                                   pan.

Dallas Country Club

(See pages 36 to 41 for
description of club and
recipes.)

BEEF ASPIC

YIELD: 2 CUPS

INGREDIENTS
Beef Stock, clarified*   2 cups
Gelatine, Unflavored   1 tbsp.

METHOD
Combine stock and gelatine; heat together 5 minutes and cool. If a thicker aspic is desired, use 1-3/4 cups stock.

*To clarify 1 qt. of stock, stir in 1 slightly beaten egg white and 1 crumbled egg shell. Without stirring, bring stock very slowly just to a simmer. Do not skim the heavy foam which comes to the surface, but make a small opening so that you can be certain stock does not boil. Simmer for 10 to 15 minutes. Remove from heat and let stand 1 hour. Push scummy crust to one side and ladle soup carefully so that it drains through a damp cloth. Cool, uncovered; store tightly covered and refrigerated.

ROUX

A roux is made by combining equal amounts of melted butter and flour; it serves as a thickening agent. A *white, or blonde, roux* is blended gently over low heat for 5 minutes in order to cook the starch, but not brown the flour. A *brown roux* should reach the color of hazelnut and smell baked, but not burned.

Wichita Country Club

(See pages 212 to 215 for description of club and recipes.)

BEURRE MANIE

YIELD: 1 CUP

INGREDIENTS

		METHOD
Butter	1/2 cup (4 oz.)	1. Combine ingredients and knead until smooth and well mixed.
Flour	3/4 cup (3 oz.)	2. Pinch off in tiny balls about the size of a pea and use for thickening sauces. The sauce should be near boiling when the Beurre Manie is added, but should cook only long enough to eliminate the raw starch taste. Prolonged cooking will cause the sauce to break or separate.
		3. Store, well covered, in the refrigerator.

PUREE OF SPLIT PEA

YIELD: 24 PORTIONS (8 oz.)

INGREDIENTS

		METHOD
Ham Shank (optional)	1	1. Put ham shank, split peas, and bay leaf in 1 gal. of water or stock and bring to boil; simmer.
Split Peas, Yellow or Green, Quick-cooking	1-1/2 lb.	
Bay Leaf	1	2. Saute salt pork to render some of the fat and then add onion and celery; cook until nearly tender. Add flour to make a roux and cook 6 minutes. Gradually stir in remaining 1/2 gallon liquid, stirring until slightly thickened and smooth. Add peas and ham shank mixture; simmer for 1 hour, or until peas are soft. Pass through a food mill or whirl in a blender. Adjust seasoning.
Water or Stock, hot	1-1/2 gal.	
Salt Pork, finely diced	1/2 lb.	
Onion, medium dice	1 lb.	
Celery, medium dice	1/2 lb.	
Flour	3/4 cup (3 oz.)	
Salt	to taste	
Pepper	to taste	

Note

For other purees, dried beans and lentils may be substituted. Soak beans overnight. Follow same procedure.

FISH STOCK

YIELD: 1-1/2 QT.

INGREDIENTS		METHOD

INGREDIENTS

Any White-fleshed Fish with Head, Bones, and Trimmings	2 lb.
Onion, Medium-sized, thinly sliced	1
Peppercorns	12
Bay Leaf	1
Thyme	1 sprig
OR	
Thyme, Dried	1/4 tsp.
Parsley	10 sprigs
Carrot, thinly sliced	1
Whole Cloves	2
Water	7 cups

METHOD

1. Place fish, onion, and peppercorns in a saucepan. Tie together with a string, the bay leaf, thyme (if fresh is used), and parsley; add, together with remaining ingredients, to the fish. Simmer gently for 1 hour. Further cooking sometimes causes bitterness.
2. Skim and strain. Cool, cover, and store in the refrigerator until used.

Note

White wine may be used for half of the liquid measure.

VARIATION: Brown fish stock may be made by browning in butter, onions, celery, and carrots (celery and carrots in an amount to equal the amount of onion); the caramelized vegetables are added to the ingredients before the stock is simmered.

BASIC FRENCH DRESSING

YIELD: 2 CUPS

INGREDIENTS
Salt   1/2 tbsp.
White Pepper   3/4 tsp.
Cider Vinegar   1/2 cup
Salad Oil   1-1/2 cups

METHOD
1. Dissolve seasonings in vinegar. Combine with oil and mix vigorously.
2. Mix well at time of use.

CREAM DRESSING FOR SALADS

YIELD: 3/4 CUP

INGREDIENTS
Cream   1/4 cup
Butter   4 tsp.
Sugar   1/3 cup
Salt   1/2 tsp.
Paprika   1/4 tsp.
Dry Mustard   1/3 tsp.
Eggs   2
Lemon Juice   1/4 cup

METHOD
1. Combine cream, butter, sugar, seasonings, and eggs in the top of a double boiler; stir and cook until thick.
2. Slowly stir in lemon juice.
3. Dressing may be thinned with additional cream or with fruit juice.

VINAIGRETTE DRESSING

YIELD: 2 CUPS

INGREDIENTS
French Dressing   2 cups
Parsley, chopped   1 tbsp.
Chives, chopped   1 tbsp.
Capers, chopped   1/2 tbsp.
Pickles, sweet, chopped 1/2 tbsp.
Egg, hard-cooked, chopped 1/2

METHOD
Combine all ingredients by shaking vigorously.

CHEESE SAUCE

YIELD:	1 CUP	1-1/2 QUARTS	
INGREDIENTS			METHOD
Butter	2 tbsp.	3/4 cup	Melt butter, remove from heat and blend in flour, salt, and pepper. Slowly stir in milk. When sauce is smooth return to heat. Stir in cheese and stir constantly until mixture simmers and thickens. Continue to cook 5 minutes or until starch flavor is gone.
Flour	2 tbsp.	3/4 cup	
Salt	1/4 tsp.	1-1/2 tsp.	
Milk	1 cup	1-1/2 qts.	
Cheddar Cheese, shredded	1 cup	6 cups	

HEAVY WHITE SAUCE

YIELD:	1/2 CUP	2 CUPS	
INGREDIENTS			METHOD
Butter	1-1/2 tbsp.	6 tbsp.	Melt butter, remove from heat and blend in flour, salt, and pepper. Slowly stir in milk. When sauce is smooth return to heat and stir constantly until mixture simmers and thickens. Continue to cook 5 minutes or until starch flavor is gone.
Flour	2 tbsp.	1/2 cup	
Salt	1/8 tsp.	1/2 tsp.	
Milk	1/2 cup	2 cups	

Beverly Hills Tennis Club

(See pages 12 to 20 for description of club and recipes.)

INDEX